SEA PRO™

Boat LURE RACKS

FIND YOUR FAVOURITE LURE AT A GLANCE

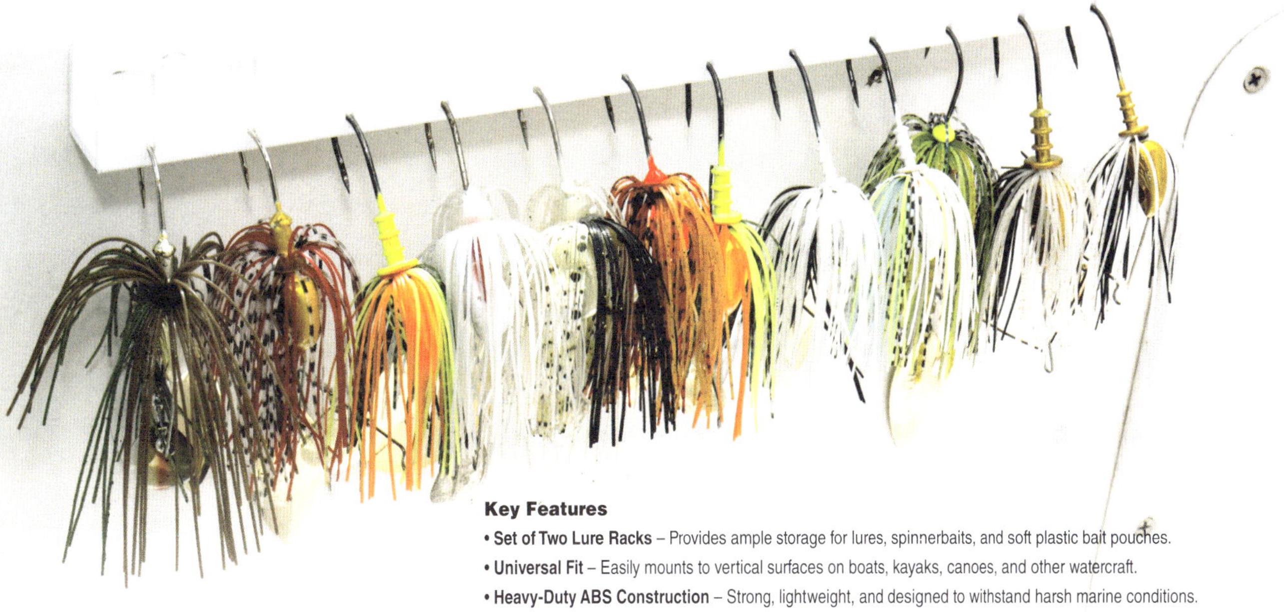

Key Features

- **Set of Two Lure Racks** – Provides ample storage for lures, spinnerbaits, and soft plastic bait pouches.
- **Universal Fit** – Easily mounts to vertical surfaces on boats, kayaks, canoes, and other watercraft.
- **Heavy-Duty ABS Construction** – Strong, lightweight, and designed to withstand harsh marine conditions.
- **Soft Plastic Pouch Holders** – Includes stainless steel holders for easy attachment of soft plastic bait pouches.

Boat CADDY ORGANISER

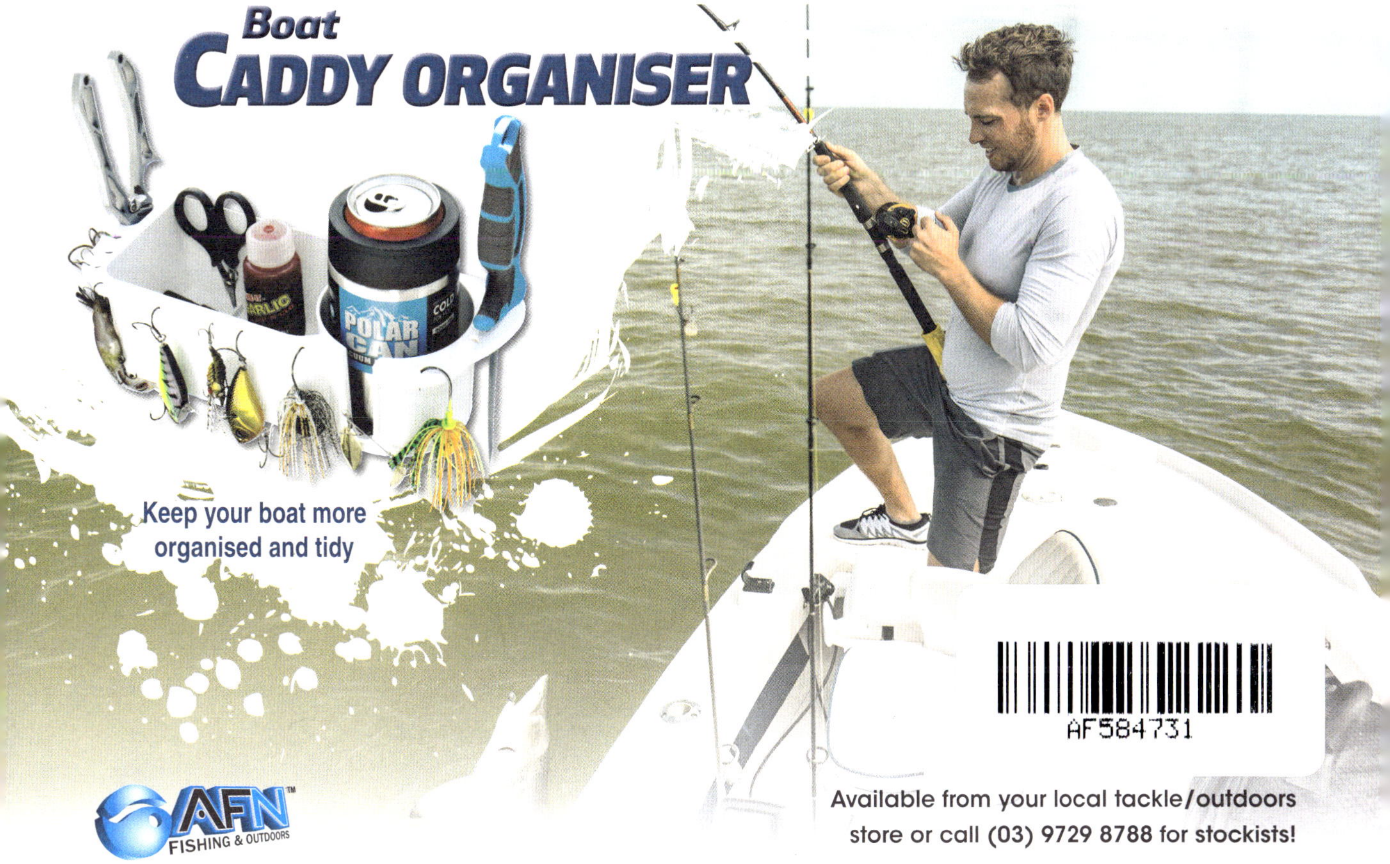

Keep your boat more organised and tidy

AF584731

Available from your local tackle/outdoors store or call (03) 9729 8788 for stockists!

AFN™ FISHING & OUTDOORS

FISHING AND CAMPING
QUEENSLAND DAMS

ROD HARRISON • BILL CLASSON • ERNIE JAMES • JASON EHRLICH

Acknowledgements - Photos

Noal Kuhl
Bill Classon
Sun Water Queensland
Rod Harrison
Les Kowitz
Jason Ehrlich
Nigel Webster
Dean Norbiato
Steve Starling
Andrew McGovern
Nick Wood
Peter Skinner
Leeann Payne

Acknowledgements - Illustrations

Trevor Hawkins

Acknowledgements - Maps

Copyright © Australian Fishing Network
All maps in this publication are based on maps from Geoscience Australia.

Cover Photos

Top Left: *Fishing the "Magic Hour" on a Queensland impoundment.*

Top Right: *Barramundi have become an important sport fishing commodity in many Queensland dams.*

Main: *Jason Ehrlich shows the type of quality bass that Queensland impoundment anglers can expect.*

Back Cover: *Weedbed barra have opened up a new world of rigs and techniques that Harro has adopted into his guiding operation.*

Fishing and Camping Queensland Dams
First published 2008
Reprinted updated and revised 2012. Reprinted 2018, 2026

Published and distributed by
AFN Fishing & Outdoors
Unit 19 & 20, 52 Corporate Blvd
Bayswater, VIC 3153
Telephone : (03) 9729 8788
Email: sales@afn.com.au
www.afn.com.au

ISBN 9 781865 132082

DISCLAIMER
Though the author and the publisher have taken care to ensure that the information contained in this publication is accurate and up to date at the time of printing they cannot take responsibility for the accuracy of information included. Camp sites can be closed at a moments notice, road conditions and vehicle requirements can change with the weather and the quality of fishing is generally dictated by seasonal conditions. It is the responsibility of readers to make contact with proper authorities prior to their departure to a particular site. Telephone numbers of the relevant authorities are provided in the text but even those are subject to change or incorrect transcription. Fishing and boating regulations are subject to change so refer to the appropriate website for the applicable legislation.

Contents

Lakes & Dams Directory

Advancetown Lake

About

Location	Nerang
Drainage	Nerang River
Surface Area	970 ha
Capacity	309,700 ML
Usage	Town Supply
Management	South East Queensland Water

Contact for fishing permit: Dam Ranger 07 5581 7645

Weipa
Cooktown
CAIRNS
TOWNSVILLE
Mount Isa
Mackay
Rockhampton
Gladstone
Bundaberg
Fraser Island
Birdsville
Maroochydore
BRISBANE
Advancetown Lake

Lake Advancetown (Hinze Dam) is situated 10 km west of Nerang on Queensland's Gold Coast. Named in honour of himself by the bulging Russ Hinze, this densely stocked water is also called Lake Advancetown, currently under construction for 3 years (until 2011). The dam wall area is closed now due to construction and an extensive prohibited area is in place. While work on the wall is being carried out there are two access points for boats. Changes can take place so check out the website for more information www.hinzedamstage3.com.

FISHING (Permit Required)

Hinze Dam has been stocked with golden perch, silver perch, saratoga, Mary River cod and Australian bass. Banded grunter have been illegally introduced and are a constant annoyance to bait anglers. Banded grunter should be destroyed if caught here.

As there are no bony bream present as forage species, many fish are prone to surface feeding, which makes this a fantastic fly fishing destination.

The main fish cover consists of the weedbeds and lily pad clusters that comprise the lake margins. Depending on water levels, Hinze has some snag habitat. These are popular with bait fishers but an early start is suggested as these are some distance from the launching ramp and electric motors aren't made for water skiing.

Catch surveys at Hinze have revealed extraordinarily high angler returns. Bass and yellowbelly dominate those statistics, along with silver perch. Growing numbers of saratoga are being encountered as the offspring of the originally stocked brood fish continue to multiply. Mary River cod are an occasional bonus catch. The electric motor rule suits trolling. Lake patrons rarely go anywhere without one or two small diving lures in trail. Though any shoreline cover is likely to harbour fish, bass and golden schools hang on the ridges where points descend to the lake floor. A motherlode at one such location produced enough fish for a win at a bass tournament some years ago, one of the last times I'd bothered about competitions.

Bass are the main sport fish in the lake.

FACILITIES

The facilities at the dam wall are currently not available. The whole area at the dam wall is closed due to works.

There is no camping permitted at Lake Advancetown. There are various accommodation options available locally. Advancetown Caravan Park 07 5533 2147

BOATING

Boaters are only allowed to use electric outboard motors on this lake and apparently, combustion motors must be removed from the hull. There are ramps at the dam wall (concrete), at the top end of the Numinbah Arm (western Arm) (dirt) and on the Little Nerang Arm (eastern arm) (gravel)—note must be 50 per cent

NOTE: The dam wall area was upgraded in 2011. Access is difficult as the dam fills and public use is expected to open in December 2011.

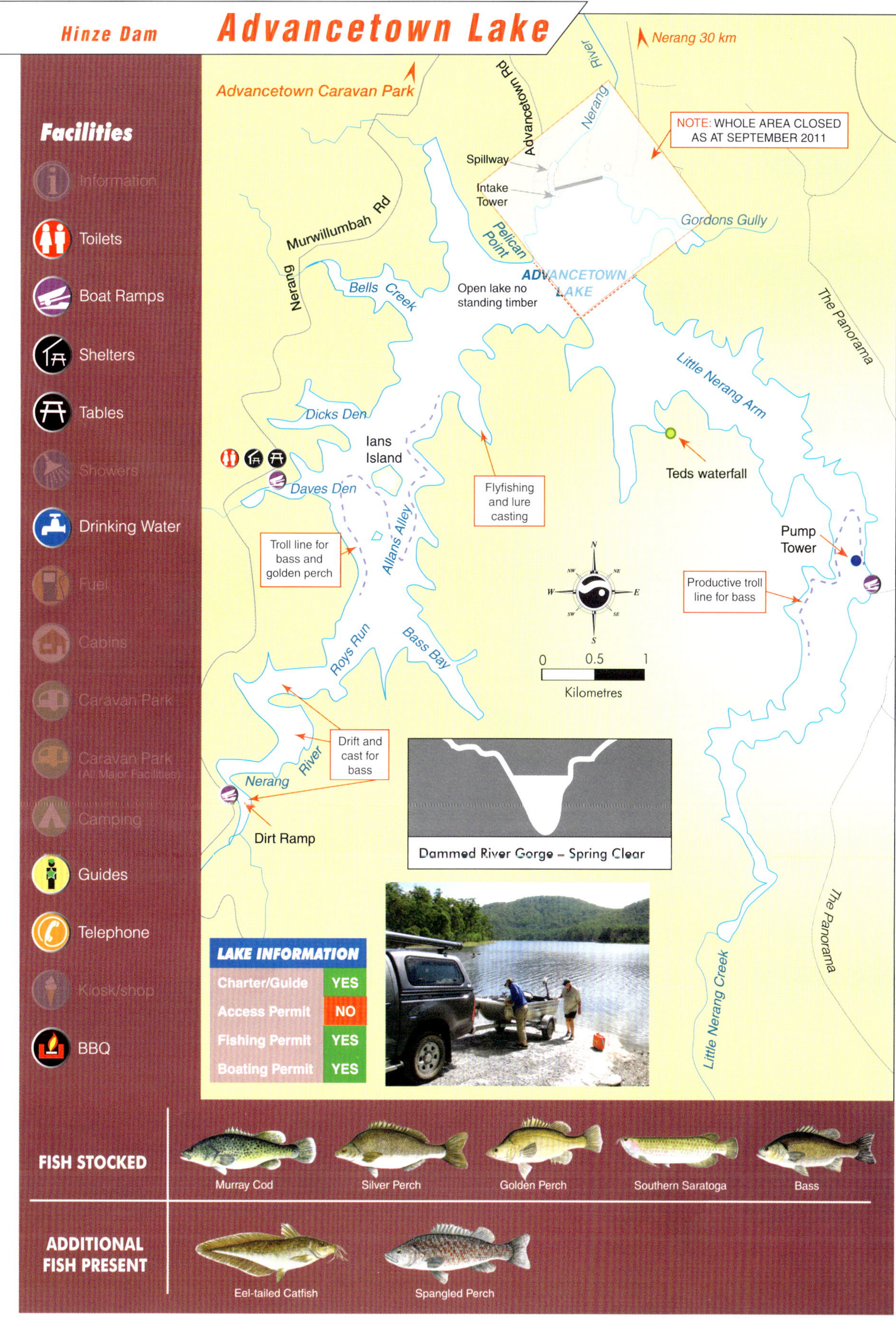

LAKE INFORMATION	
Charter/Guide	YES
Access Permit	NO
Fishing Permit	YES
Boating Permit	YES

Atkinson Dam

About

Location	Lowood
Drainage	Buaraba Creek
Surface Area	550 ha
Capacity	30,500 ML
Usage	Irrigation
Management	Sun Water 07 3884 5317

Contact for fishing permit: N/A

Weipa
Cooktown
CAIRNS
TOWNSVILLE
Mount Isa
Mackay
Rockhampton
Gladstone
Bundaberg
Fraser Island
Birdsville
Maroochydore
Atkinson Dam
BRISBANE

Originally a natural lagoon that filled from Brisbane River flooding, the construction of the wall in 1970 resulted in a considerably increased capacity. Previous fish stocks are likely to have been lost when the basin of the lake went dry due to severe drought. Since then, the lake has filled but as Atkinsons Dam isn't part of the Stocked Impoundment Permit system no further stockings have been carried out. There is talk of a local business getting behind a stocking program. After the hard work of others we may be able to enjoy this lake again in the future.

The waters are mainly used for irrigation of the extensive market garden agriculture and cereal crops grown in the region. Those water requirements, which peak during summer, exacerbate the drawdown rate. Besides curtailing bank fishing and boating, lowering waters suffer a commensurate oxygen loss. The biology of native fish from the Murray Darling system have evolved to cope with such conditions but there are limits. Yellowbelly in particular have the capacity to "wind back" metabolism during dry times, taking nutrition by re-absorbing body fat accumulated during better times. When low water conditions set in and that biological train is in motion fish go "doggo" and become difficult, if not impossible, to catch. Fish native to coastal river systems, which generally have watersheds where rains are more reliable, are not as resilient when it comes to low, de-

A misty morning on Atkinson Dam.

A yellowbelly about to be returned to the water.

oxygenated water.

FISHING (Permit Required)

Atkinson's Dam has been privately stocked with southern strain saratoga that were growing strongly prior to the collapse of water levels. It is very much doubtful if they will survive till meaningful rains return. And when better conditions prevailed, the golden and silver perch also numbered amongst catches. Being on the eastern side of the range, Atkinson's Dam has the potential to hold bass, golden perch, silver perch, saratoga and Mary River cod. While it would be great to see these species in the lake, a repeat of the dry times in previous years is a serious concern.

BOATING

A boating permit is required and authorities allow no more than 15 boats on the lake at any one time.

FACILITIES

Excellent facilities include Atkinson Dam Waterfront Caravan Park 07 5426 4151, and Atkinson Dam Cabin Village 07 5426 4211 permanent and overnight vans, cabins, powered and bush camping sites, kiosk and a bush kitchen. Pets are welcome.

Atkinson Dam

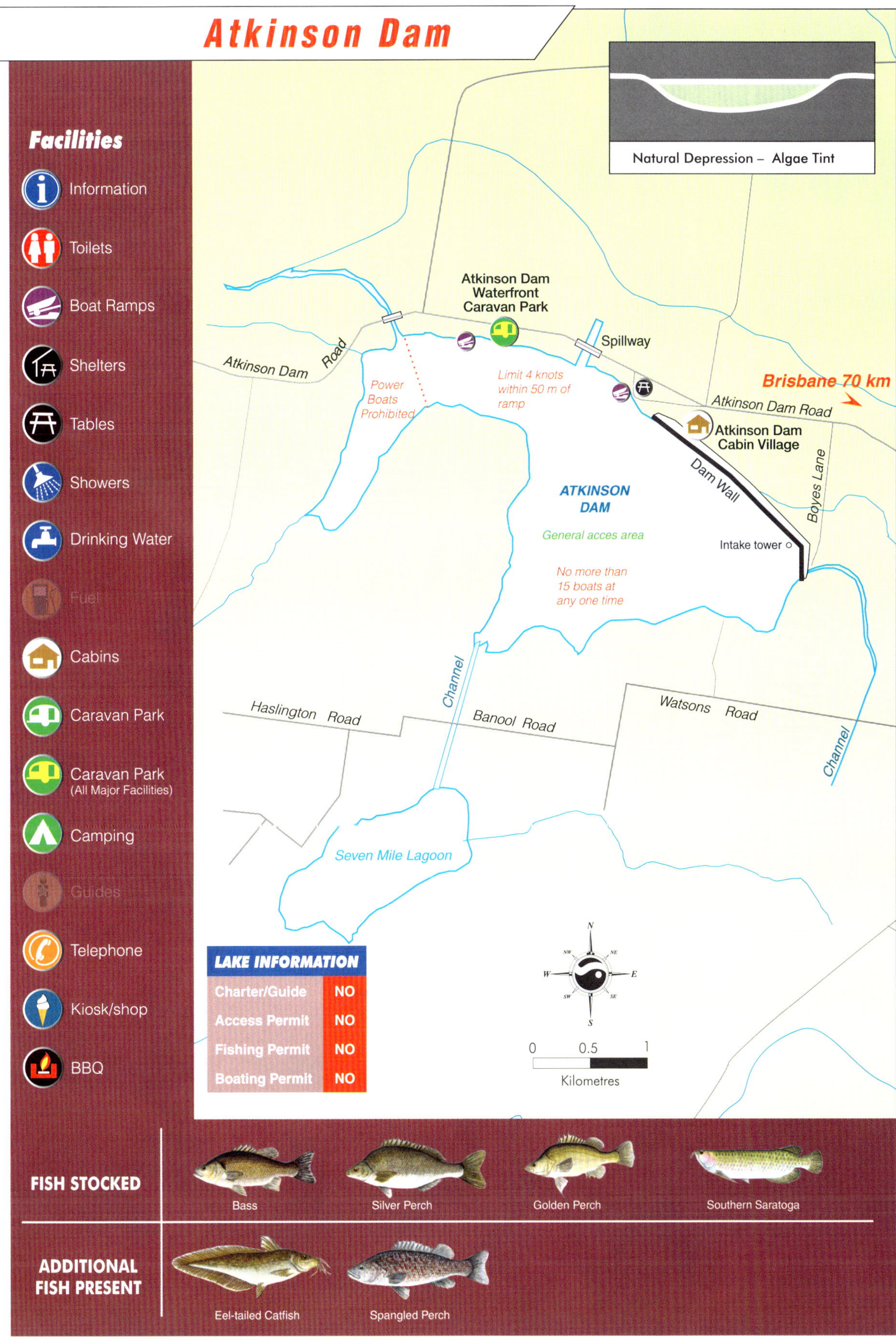

LAKE INFORMATION	
Charter/Guide	NO
Access Permit	NO
Fishing Permit	NO
Boating Permit	NO

Awoonga Dam

About

Location	Gladstone
Drainage	Fitzroy Region
Surface Area	6750 ha
Capacity	777,000 ML
Usage	Town Water & Industry
Management	Gladston Area Water Board (Ranger 0419 661 482)

Contact for fishing permit: N/A

Australia's premier big barra fishery is well signposted and attracts visitors from far and wide. Awoonga serves domestic, industrial and recreational needs of the region and hosts extensive and well maintained facilities. Show piece water, you can be sure—Awoonga enjoys advantages over other stocked fisheries—its own hatchery and no SIP permit.

As part of a significant contribution to regional tourism and quality of life for local citizenry, the Gladstone Area Water Board fully funds fisherfolk.

A walk through shady visitor parklands is likely to reveal slumbering pretty face wallabies, otherwise rare. The lake and environs are a bird watcher's delight—waterfowl, waders and raptors.

Major flooding in 2010/2011 saw Awoonga Dam well above capacity and pouring water over the spillway. The result was thousands of escaped barra which made their way into the Boyne River system below. This great escape created its own awesome barramundi fishery in the waters below the dam. Stocking statistics show there to be plenty of barra left in the lake and with their own barra hatchery there is no doubting that Awoonga Dam will retain its crown as the states premier impoundment barra fishery.

FISHING

Nearly three million barra fingerlings have been released and in a most exciting development, growing numbers of mangrove jacks. Encounters with 80 cm / 8 kg fish are reminiscent of days on hand to hand combat with its close relative the Papuan black bass. Awoonga is a classic example of a eutrophic lake. The open spaces and shallow fringes encourage prolific water plant growths, which in turn form the basis of a dense and diverse food chain biomass.

Trolling at night is popular and the most productive method, but there are big barra that fall regularly to lure casting.

Predatory fish eat more while expending less energy in the hunt. Weight gain is therefore more rapid and pronounced than with free range fish. The scenic backdrop of Mount Castletower and associated peaks enhances the Awoonga big barra magnetism.

FACILITIES

The Lake Awoonga Caravan Park, 07 4975 0033, features powered and non powered caravan and camp sites, as well as cabins. There are also toilets, barbecues, drinking water, playgrounds, tables and a kiosk and restaurant.

Only five minutes away is Awoonga Gateway Lodge, 07 4975 0033. These comfortable cabins are fully self contained and are a great place to relax between fishing sessions.

Awoonga Houseboats, 07 4975 0930, offer several vessels from kayaks right through to the 43 foot houseboat the Barra Queen which sleeps ten.

BOATING

There are no restrictions except for jet skis. There is a wide, concrete single ramp that can take two boats at a time if care is taken.

A barra explosion on Awoonga Dam.

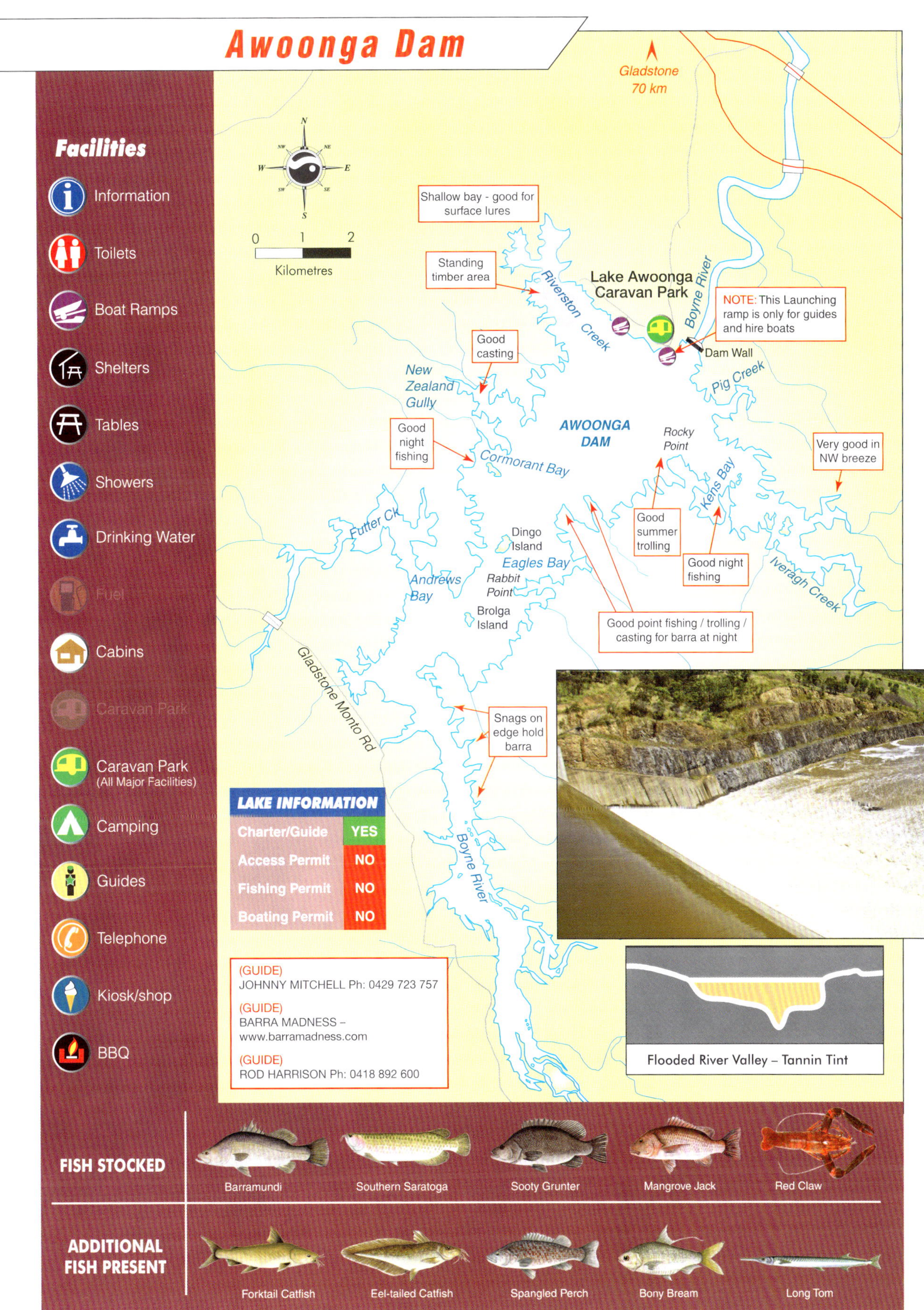
Awoonga Dam
Facilities
Information
Toilets
Boat Ramps
Shelters
Tables
Showers
Drinking Water
Fuel
Cabins
Caravan Park
Caravan Park (All Major Facilities)
Camping
Guides
Telephone
Kiosk/shop
BBQ
N
NE
E
SE
S
SW
W
NW
0 1 2
Kilometres
Gladstone 70 km
Shallow bay - good for surface lures
Standing timber area
Riverston Creek
Lake Awoonga Caravan Park
Boyne River
NOTE: This Launching ramp is only for guides and hire boats
Dam Wall
Good casting
New Zealand Gully
Pig Creek
AWOONGA DAM
Rocky Point
Very good in NW breeze
Good night fishing
Cormorant Bay
Kens Bay
Futter Ck
Dingo Island
Good summer trolling
Eagles Bay
Good night fishing
Andrews Bay
Rabbit Point
Iveragh Creek
Brolga Island
Good point fishing / trolling / casting for barra at night
Gladstone Monto Rd
Snags on edge hold barra
Boyne River
LAKE INFORMATION
Charter/Guide YES
Access Permit NO
Fishing Permit NO
Boating Permit NO
(GUIDE)
JOHNNY MITCHELL Ph: 0429 723 757
(GUIDE)
BARRA MADNESS – www.barramadness.com
(GUIDE)
ROD HARRISON Ph: 0418 892 600
Flooded River Valley – Tannin Tint
FISH STOCKED
Barramundi
Southern Saratoga
Sooty Grunter
Mangrove Jack
Red Claw
ADDITIONAL FISH PRESENT
Forktail Catfish
Eel-tailed Catfish
Spangled Perch
Bony Bream
Long Tom

Baroon Pocket Dam

About

Location	Maleny
Drainage	Obi Obi Creek
Surface Area	400 ha
Capacity	61,000 ML
Usage	Town Water
Management	Caloundra Maroochy Water Supply Board

Contact for fishing permit: 07 5445 0956 (on-site registration)

This little publicised fishery nestles in Sunshine Coast hinterland hills. Constructed in 1988 on Obi Obi Creek, an upper Mary River tributary, Lake Baroon—to cite a local abbreviation—is a domestic storage for the Caloundra/Maroochydore region. It is situated 7 km north east of Maleny and 5 km south west of Montville. Of academic interest as they are totally protected, is that Obi Obi Gorge, located below the dam, remains one of the few locations where Mary River Cod are maintaining a wild population. The terrain there is, fortunately, for young legs and a spirit of adventure. By and large, those who go to the trouble to get there now abide by the ban.

FISHING (Permit Required)

Apart from a stand of timber (to which access is restricted), the lake is devoid of obvious hard cover. This places a priority on any sunken snags anglers may discover. Extensive weed margins exclude shoreline fishing. Best techniques include trolling, casting to weed edges and pocket and vertical presentations to fish holding on deep features such as the edges of former creek beds.

Lake Baroon is primarily a bass fishery. However, sizes have plummeted to the extent that 40 cm fish aren't common. This trend may be attributable to a lack of bony bream and some shocking bag limit abuses during the first years following stocking. Golden perch and silver perch have also been stocked. Mary River cod, eel-tailed catfish and spangled perch are also present. There is a ban on the use of lead sinkers.

FACILITIES

Sealed ramp. No facilities, no camping. Accommodation in nearby Montville and Maleny, there is a caravan park in Maleny.

BOATING

No fossil fuel motors are allowed on the lake. Electric motors are allowed on dinghies, but not on canoes. A maximum of ten electric powered craft are permitted on the water at any one time. A boating permit currently costing $5/day or $50/year is required. These are available on site.

As Lake Baroon is small by impoundment standards, kayaking is the perfect way to fish these waters.

Baroon Pocket Dam

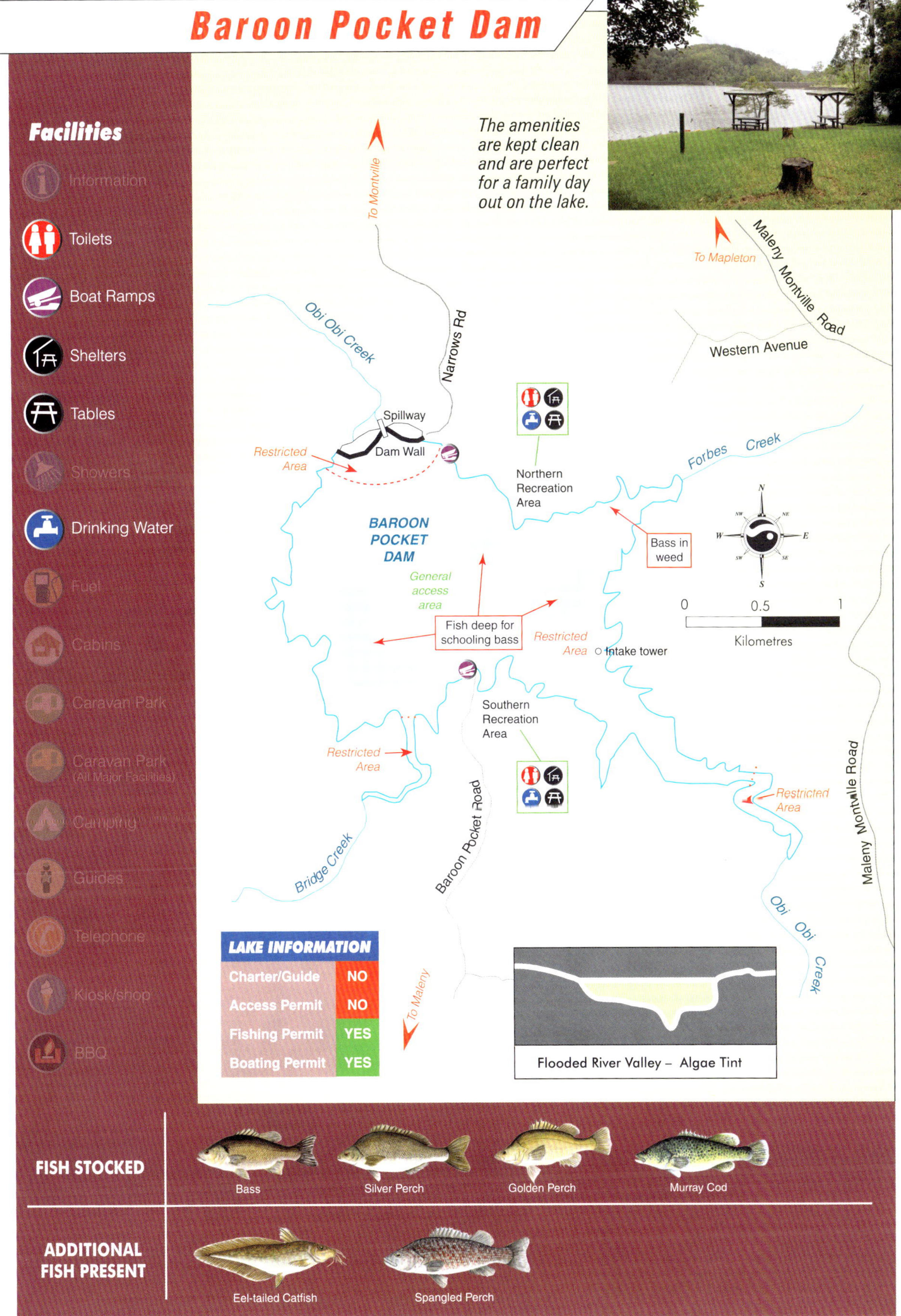

LAKE INFORMATION	
Charter/Guide	NO
Access Permit	NO
Fishing Permit	YES
Boating Permit	YES

Bjelke Petersen Dam

About

Location	Murgon
Drainage	Barker Creek
Surface Area	2150 ha
Capacity	125,000 ML
Usage	Irrigation
Management	Sun Water 07 4132 6200

Contact for fishing permit: www.smartservice.qld.gov.au or Sun Water

Named after an original property in the region, Lake Barambah is also called Bjelke-Petersen Dam after Queensland's late Premier. An earth and rock fill structure with a central clay core, the dam wall's engineering specs are 540 m long, a maximum height of 34 m, and a 135 m thickness at the base. The lake has a generally shallow basin that's fringed with weedbeds along with snaggy sections towards the lake back blocks.

FISHING (Permit Required)

Lake Barambah has been stocked with golden perch, silver perch, saratoga and Australian bass. There are breeding populations of Tandans (eel-tailed catfish) and spangled perch here as well as the illegally introduced sleepy cod and redclaw crayfish.

Once overshadowed by the likes of lakes Somerset and Wivenhoe, Lake Barambah has come of age in the last few years and is now regarded as one of the big bass impoundments in Queensland.

When full, an exposed hump towards the rear of the main basin bears the somewhat prophetic title of Treasure Island. BP—a much used abbreviation—has been a bass fishery of note that's produced many 50 cm class fish over the years. Richly coloured golden perch and stud silver perch are also amongst the BP bounty. The generally shallow nature of the lake, combined with some regional rain shadow, results in severe shrinkage of the surface area during summer. That of '07 saw the lake retreat into the former creek beds. By the start of 2011 the dam was full. This extra water will be a boost to the ecosystem and see fingerlings grow at fast rates to quickly reach legal size. With no significant catchment from which to fill, locals need to brush up on their rain dance. Small diving lures with 2–4 m depth capabilities are popular with trollers. Casting anglers do well on all major species with spinnerbaits.

FACILITIES

Camping is permitted on site with limited cabins available at the Yallakool Tourist Park, 07 4168 4746. There are other tourist parks and hotel / motel style accommodation close by in Murgon.

BOATING

There are normally no boating restrictions on Lake Barambah. There is a no boating / fishing zone in front of the dam wall. There are two boat ramps provided, one adjacent to the dam wall and another immediately below the camping area.

Boating aplenty on Bjelke Petersen Dam.

Lake Barambah Bjelke Petersen Dam

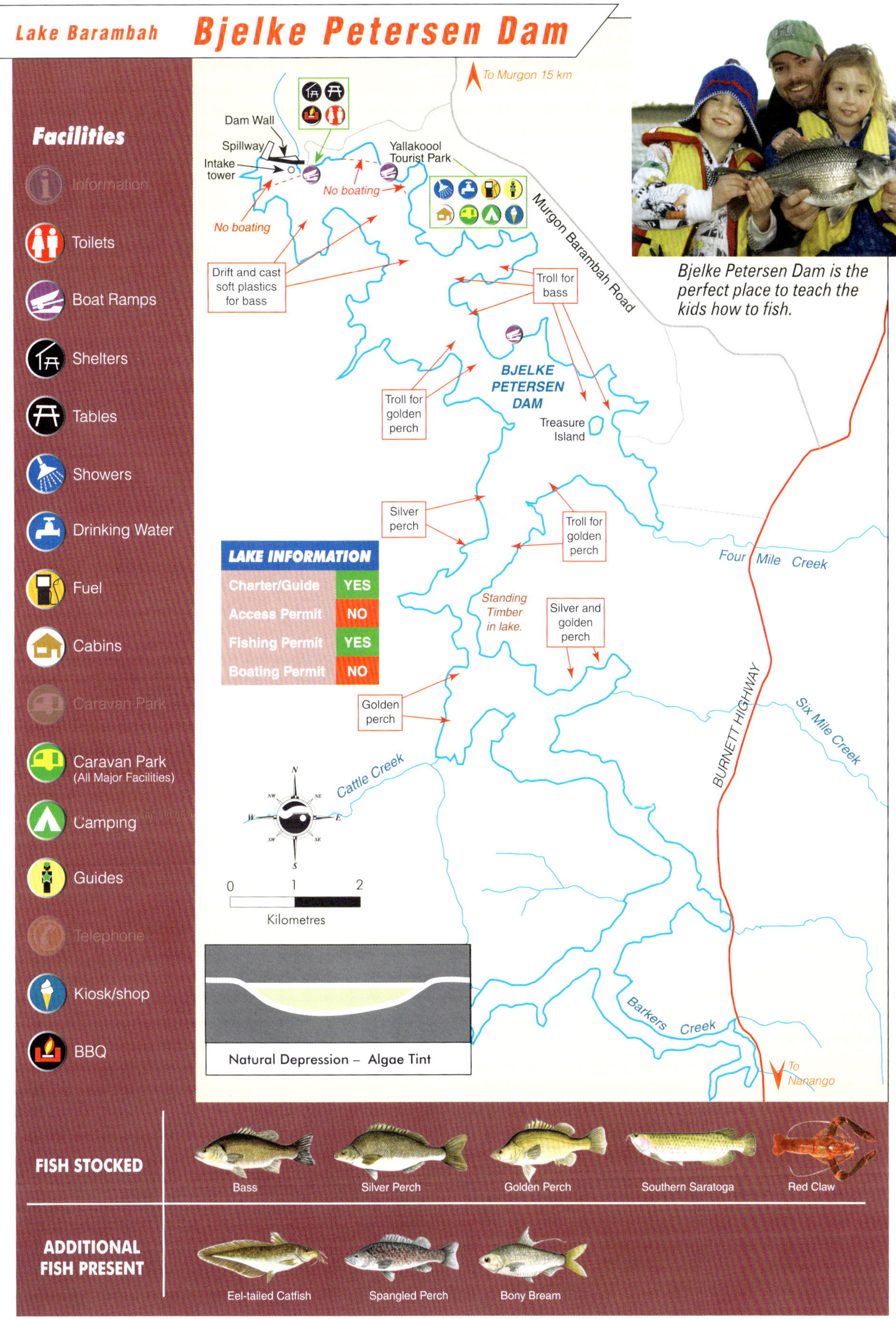

LAKE INFORMATION	
Charter/Guide	YES
Access Permit	NO
Fishing Permit	YES
Boating Permit	NO

Bjelke Petersen Dam is the perfect place to teach the kids how to fish.

Boondooma Lake

Weipa
Cooktown
CAIRNS
TOWNSVILLE
Mount Isa
Mackay
Rockhampton
Gladstone
Bundaberg
Fraser Island
Birdsville
Boondooma Lake
Maroochydore
BRISBANE

About

Location	Proston
Drainage	Stuart System
Surface Area	1920 ha
Capacity	210,000 ML
Usage	Domestic Agriculture / Power
Management	Sun Water 07 4132 6200

Contact for fishing permit: www.smartservice.qld.gov.au or Sun Water

Located around 20 km north west of Proston and 75 km from Kingaroy, Boondooma Dam is a leisurely three and a half hour drive north west of Brisbane.

The Boondooma Dam was constructed in 1983 across the Boyne river below it's confluence with the Stuart to supply water to the Tarong power station and as is the case at so many impoundments, takes its name from the original property in the area.

FISHING (Permit Required)

Boondooma has had a very mixed stocking history, being one of the only impoundments to be stocked with both Murray cod and Mary River cod in the past as well as the continued stocking of bass, golden perch, silver perch and saratoga. There is also a naturally occurring population of Tandans (eel-tailed catfish) and spangled perch.

In 1993/94 approximately 60–65,000 barramundi were released into Boondooma as it was felt that this was possibly the furthest south that barra could survive. To date there have been only a couple of reported captures here and since then no further barra releases have taken place. Since that time, barramundi have been a hit at lakes at the same latitude but closer to the coast.

The backed up waters fork into two arms, one where standing timber predominates with the other containing prominent rip-rap and other rocky outcrops. The stocking history includes Murray cod—both western rivers stain and Mary River cod. These will interbreed to produce hybrids. Barramundi were also trialled but failed. Significantly, Lake Awoonga—barra central—is sited further down the Boyne River. A high level of baitfishing occurs at Boondooma with stocking densities adjusted in favour of the ten fish bag limit on golden perch. Shrimps are the preferred bait and regulars have their favourite trees. A more recent, an unfortunate introduction has been tilapia. If you catch one of these pest fish, please destroy it. They find favour as a table fish with yokels and others responsible for their illegal spread.

Boondooma has become a lake that's fully utilised fish-wise. Stocking densities are commensurate with extraction rates. This dynamic may not be conducive to the development of a trophy fishery, but it goes some way towards being able to take home a feed of yellowbelly.

Schooling bass can be found throughout the lake. In winter these fish tend to migrate up the lake's two arms to just before the start of the timber. As conditions warm, schools tend to form in the main basin closer to the dam wall. Boondooma's bass are suckers for soft plastics and ice jigs.

During the cooler months, it's worth prospecting around the weedy edges of the lake with spinnerbaits, lipless cranks, soft plastics and blade baits for a mixed bag of bass and golden perch. In summer the fish can scatter making lure trolling the best option, ensuring plenty of water is covered.

FACILITIES

The Lake Boondooma Camping & Recreation Area, 07 4168 9694, features self-contained cabins, a modern caravan park with powered sites and unpowered lakeside camping. It has modern amenity blocks, wood and electric barbecues, safe children's playground, multiple picnic areas around the lake foreshores and a centrally-located kiosk

BOATING

There is a good quality, two lane boat ramp. There are normally no boating restrictions on Lake Boondooma, however there is a no fishing / boating zone around the dam wall. Boats of 4 hp and 6 hp are available for hire.

Casting amongst the timber can be productive.

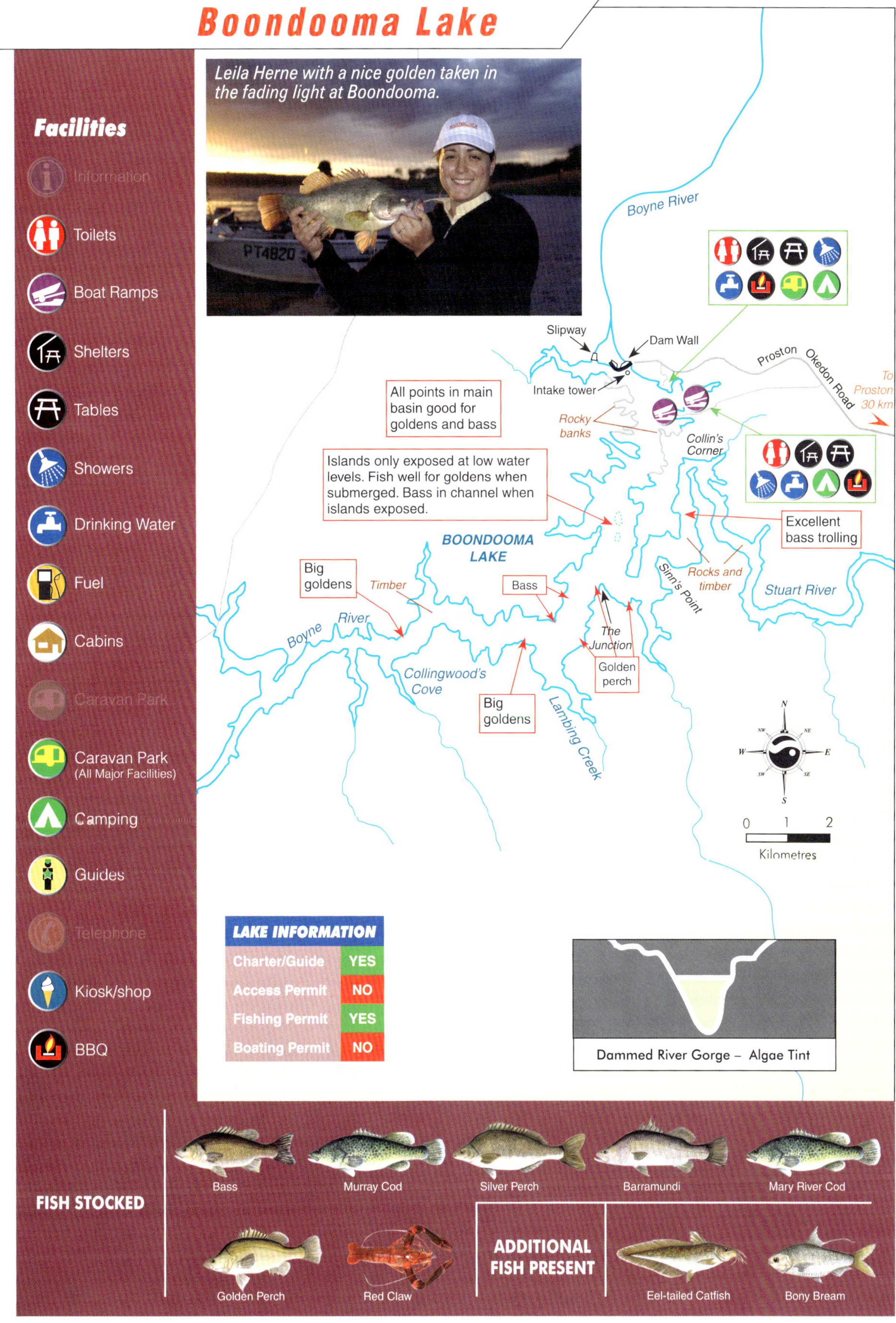

Boondooma Lake
Leila Herne with a nice golden taken in the fading light at Boondooma.
Facilities
Information
Toilets
Boat Ramps
Shelters
Tables
Showers
Drinking Water
Fuel
Cabins
Caravan Park
Caravan Park (All Major Facilities)
Camping
Guides
Telephone
Kiosk/shop
BBQ
Boyne River
Slipway
Dam Wall
Intake tower
Proston Okedon Road
To Proston 30 km
All points in main basin good for goldens and bass
Rocky banks
Collin's Corner
Islands only exposed at low water levels. Fish well for goldens when submerged. Bass in channel when islands exposed.
Excellent bass trolling
BOONDOOMA LAKE
Big goldens
Timber
Bass
Sinn's Point
Rocks and timber
Stuart River
Boyne River
The Junction
Golden perch
Collingwood's Cove
Big goldens
Lambing Creek
N
S
E
W
NW
NE
SW
SE
0 1 2
Kilometres
LAKE INFORMATION
Charter/Guide YES
Access Permit NO
Fishing Permit YES
Boating Permit NO
Dammed River Gorge – Algae Tint
FISH STOCKED
Bass
Murray Cod
Silver Perch
Barramundi
Mary River Cod
Golden Perch
Red Claw
ADDITIONAL FISH PRESENT
Eel-tailed Catfish
Bony Bream

Borumba Dam

About

Location	Imbil – Sunshine Coast
Drainage	Mary River
Surface Area	500 ha
Capacity	33,300 ML
Usage	Irrigation
Management	Sun Water 07 4132 6200

Contact for fishing permit: www.smartservice.qld.gov.au or Sun Water

Weipa
Cooktown
CAIRNS
TOWNSVILLE
Mount Isa
Mackay
Rockhampton
Gladstone
Bundaberg
Fraser Island
Birdsville
Borumba Dam
Maroochydore
BRISBANE

This picture postcard lake was constructed in 1964 on Yabba Creek (a cloistered, fish filled, upper Mary River tributary ideal for yak fishing). Misty Borumba mornings are good times to be alive—red deer grazing at the water's edge, dingo howls in the hills and the saratoga rising. The first lake to be stocked, Borumba was seeded with southern saratoga by Hamar Midgeley, who later did work on Nile perch, a one-time candidate for Queensland's lakes. Borumba now holds a mother lode of these challenging and entertaining fish. Progressive enlargement works have increased the lake capacity.

FISHING (Permit Required)

Saratoga attract a constant stream of fly and lure anglers and can be taken on a year round basis. Being such an awful table fish places them beyond the attentions of bait fishermen interested in take-home fish. Yellowbelly and silver perch have been stocked in viable numbers and, in more recent years, bass. Trolling in the main basin—open water popular with water skiers at weekends—is productive for anglers just wishing to kick back. The upper lake forks into two heavily timbered arms where saratoga lurk. Sportfishers mooch around those reaches on electric motors casting small lures and flies. If silence is golden, it's priceless around 'toga.

FACILITIES

A camping ground (unpowered sites) with an ablution block is sited on Yabba Creek, below the dam wall. Enquiries and bookings 07 5482 2555. Powered caravans and sites are available at Borumba Deer Park 07 5484 5196, 2 km from the lake on the access road.

BOATING

A calm, misty Borumba morning is good for the soul. There are no boating restrictions though courtesy and common sense can become casualties on a busy powerboat weekend.

A misty Borumba morning is prime time to tangle with feisty lake residents.

Borumba Dam

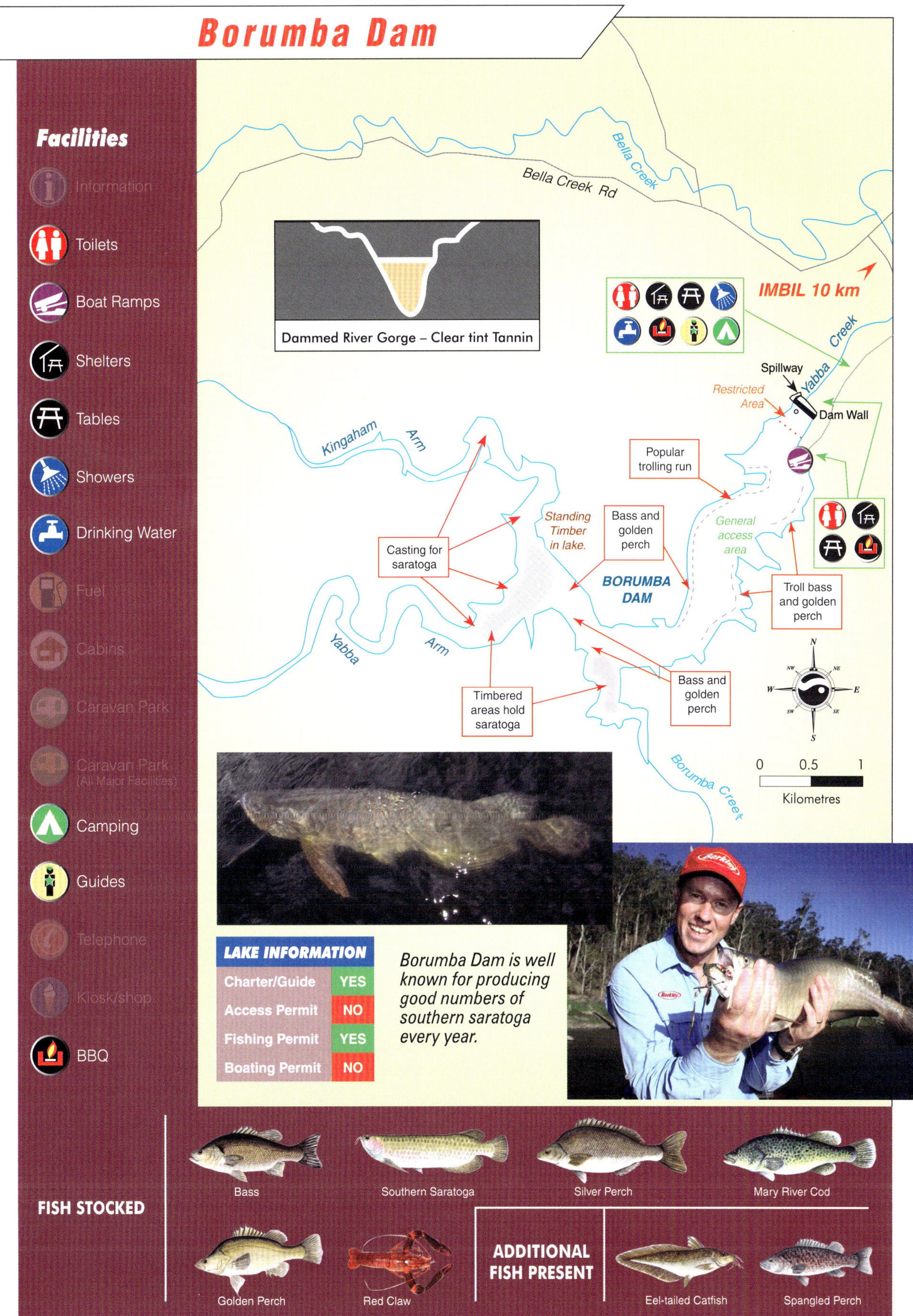

LAKE INFORMATION	
Charter/Guide	YES
Access Permit	NO
Fishing Permit	YES
Boating Permit	NO

Borumba Dam is well known for producing good numbers of southern saratoga every year.

Bundoora Dam

About

Location	Middlemount
Drainage	Fitzroy River
Surface Area	460 ha
Capacity	10,000 ML
Usage	Industrial
Management	Broadsound Shire Council

Contact for fishing permit: Broadsound Shire Council 07 4964 5400

This is a relatively new lake has been waiting to happen. The portion of German Creek, an upper feeder of the vast Fitzroy, it now fills is dished landform that was transformed into a lake pretty much using equipment used in conjunction with local open cut coal mines. In fact, the purpose of Bundoora is to supply water to those operations. A downside takes the form of rapid drawdowns when demands peak. Substantial drops in water level tend not be so obvious in steep sided lakes.

FISHING (Permit Required)

A naturally occurring yellowbelly stock along with a few saratoga are amongst original inhabitants. Also present are eel-tailed catfish, sleepy cod, spangled perch and redclaw crayfish. Fishing pressures are light but will increase as barramundi stockings mature. The relative open nature of the lake will favour trolling. However, skilled casters will get just rewards through working the lake edges. Shoreline casting is effective, especially around dusk and after, when feeding barramundi move into the shallower lake fringes. Selecting the right lure is important—one that has the weight necessary for long casts yet does not dive deeply into waiting weeds.

FACILITIES

Camping is permitted but facilities are sparse. Fixtures include picnic tables and toilets. Enquiries at Bundoora Recreational Fishing Club, Private Mail Bag, Middlemount, Qld, 4746.

BOATING

A boating speed limit of 6 knots applies throughout the lake.

Naturally occurring golden perch.

Bundoora Dam

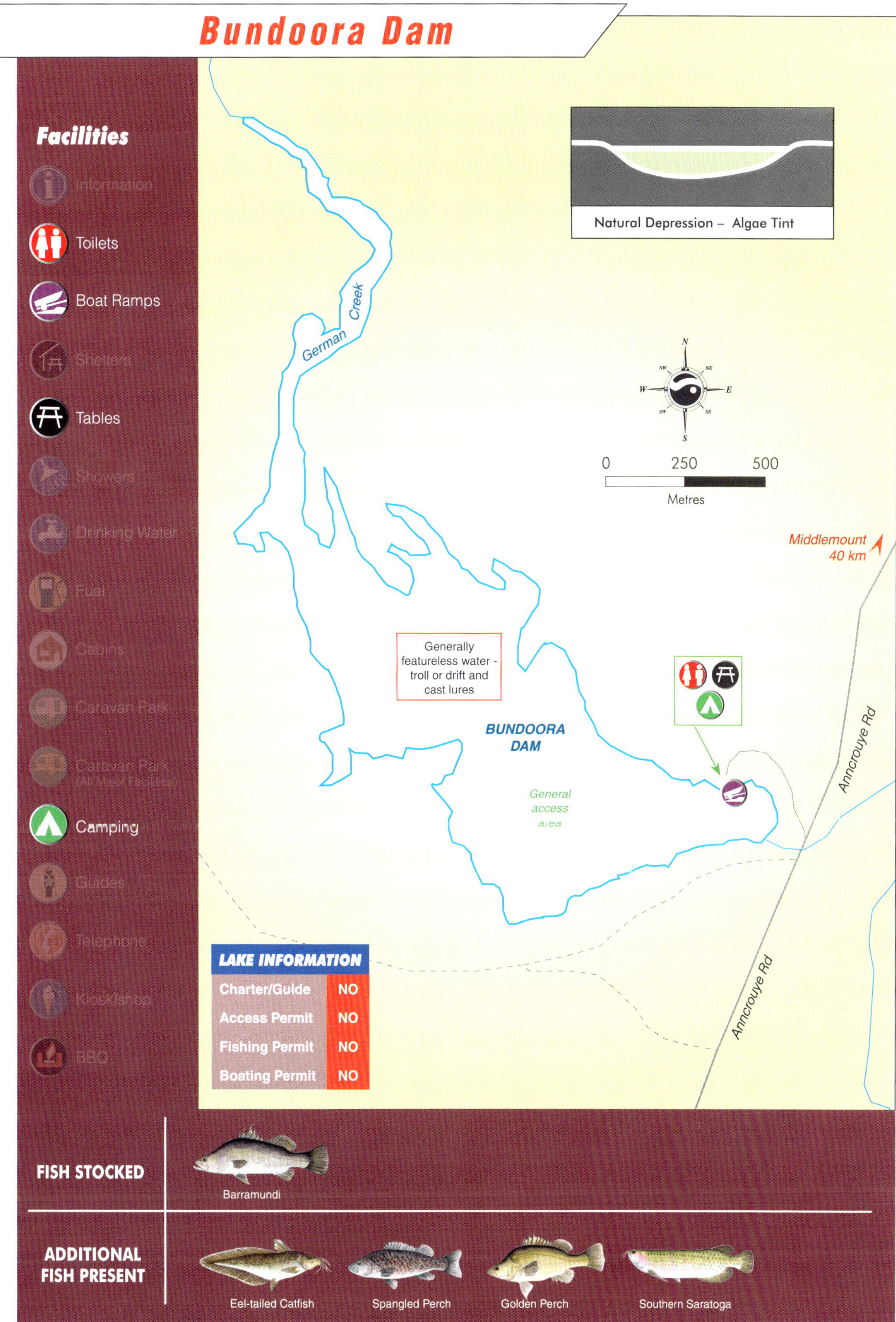

LAKE INFORMATION	
Charter/Guide	NO
Access Permit	NO
Fishing Permit	NO
Boating Permit	NO

FISH STOCKED

Barramundi

ADDITIONAL FISH PRESENT

Eel-tailed Catfish
Spangled Perch
Golden Perch
Southern Saratoga

Callide Dam

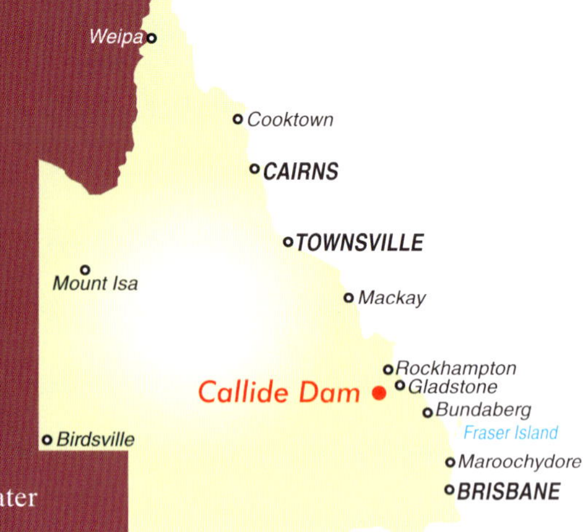

About

Location	Biloela
Drainage	Dawson River
Surface Area	1250 ha
Capacity	135,000 ML
Usage	Industrial
Management	Sun Water 07 4992 8111

Contact for fishing permit: www.smartservice.qld.gov.au or Sun Water

Barramundi are thriving in Callide Dam thanks to active stocking groups.

Built on upper Callide Creek, a Dawson River tributary 20 km east of Biloela, this lake has a primary function of supplying cooling waters for the nearby coal burning power station. Both station and lake are linked to industry in the Gladstone region. At peak capacity, Callide is a relatively shallow lake, 10 metres deep at the wall, and averaging about 4 metres through most of the rest. Save for a few rocky points and the odd stick, it is a somewhat featureless lake.

FISHING (Permit Required)

Callide is one of Queensland's latest barra fisheries and is fast making a name for itself. A well resourced regional economy and an active stocking group has resulted in dense stocking levels and the combination of more fish mixed with less water has meant happy barra days. The association operates its own hatchery.

The combination of low water and a chillier than usual '07 winter brought on a massive fish kill. And in the vein that fish can keep growing after their demise, the stories circulating put it at biblical proportions. Anyway, the locals simply cleaned up the mess and 'got on with it'. Fears that the entire barra stock was lost are diluted at this autumn '08 writing. Callide is still producing barra and with restocking ramping up, seasonal aberrations will fade. The fish stocking groups gives quite a few barra fingerlings an even better chance of survival by putting them into grow out ponds. Here, with no predators, the fish can grow before being released giving them a much better chance of survival.

Saratoga have been doing well and are such a common bycatch by barra anglers that they could be specifically targeted with success.

FACILITIES

There is no camping at the lake but there is camping, a caravan park and motel accommodation at Biloela. There are toilets, barbecues, drinking water and picnic tables at the lake.

BOATING

There are no restrictions except for a 200 metre no-go zone from the spillway. The boat ramps are concrete.

Callide Dam

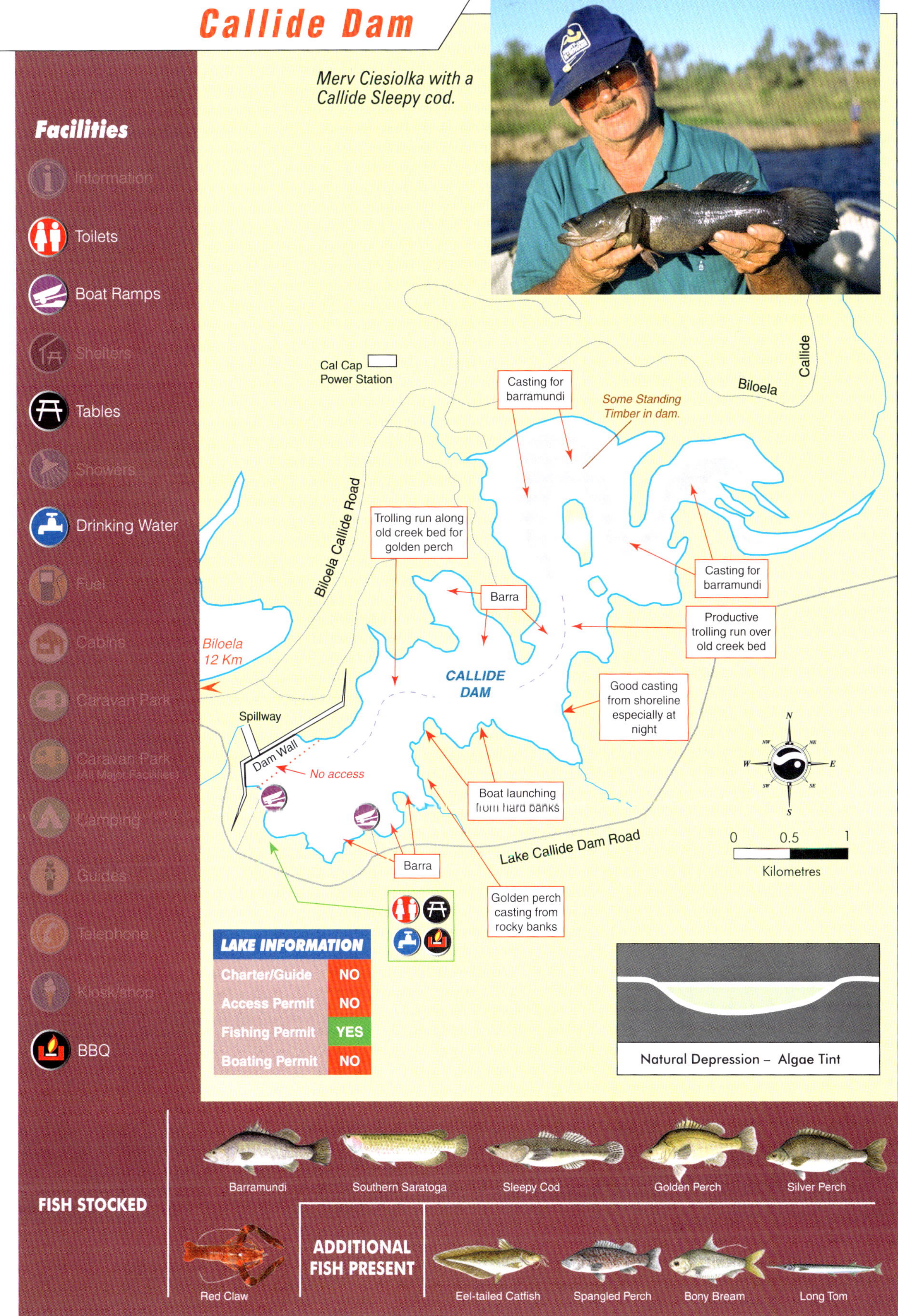

Merv Ciesiolka with a Callide Sleepy cod.

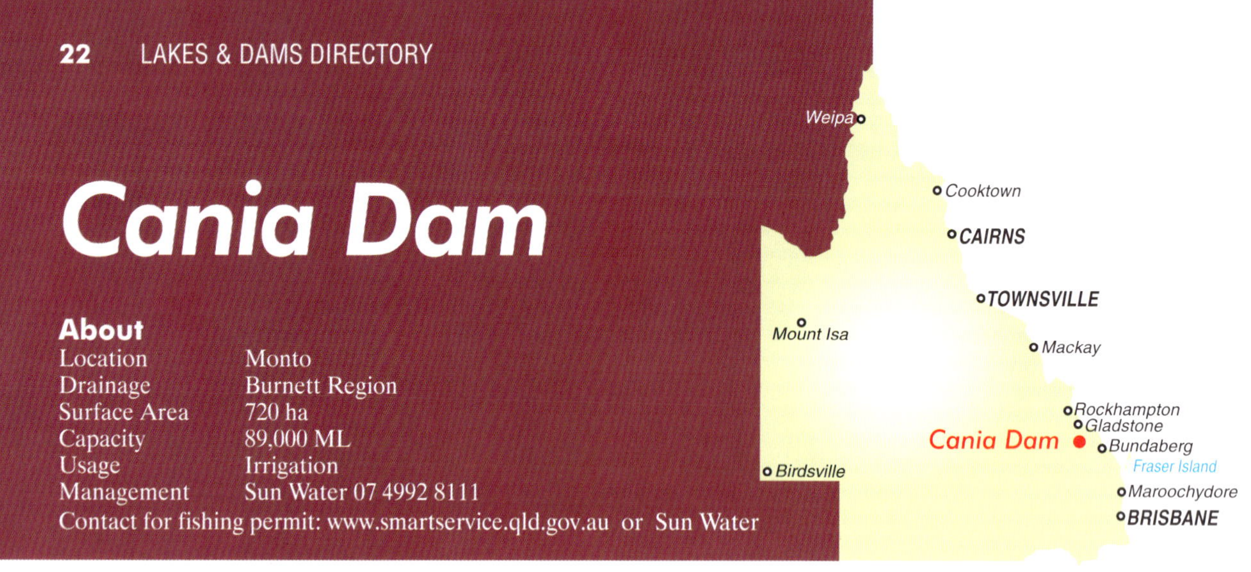

Cania Dam

About

Location	Monto
Drainage	Burnett Region
Surface Area	720 ha
Capacity	89,000 ML
Usage	Irrigation
Management	Sun Water 07 4992 8111

Contact for fishing permit: www.smartservice.qld.gov.au or Sun Water

Fishing tight against the banks is a popular approach at Cania Dam.

Built in 1982, within sight of spectacular Cania Gorge on Three Moon Creek, an upper Burnett River feeder, Cania has a special significance. It was the first lake anywhere to be stocked with hatchery bred bass, a fish no one wanted. The result of a private hatchery breakthrough by Bill Proctor and Will Truman, but for the initiative of Monto angler John Henderson pouring those 30,000 fingerlings into Cania, nothing would have happened. Saratoga were transported overland from the Dawson River, not that far as the crow flies. Golden and silver perch were later added to the mix. Overall, Cania is a bland looking lake.

The foreshore of what can be considered the main basin is steep sided and stony. Then, as one progresses up the lake, the landform gives way to flatlands where cattle graze. And finally, should that lake level be sufficiently high, there's a timbered back block that offers visible hard cover.

FISHING (Permit Required)

Casting has always been more effective in Cania than trolling. Spinnerbaits can and do catch everything swimming in the lake. Small minnow types are also effective. Casting lures can be trolled using an electric motor with great success. Lipless crankbaits, spinnerbaits, blades and soft plastics can all be trolled at around 2 to 3 km/h. By altering the speed and varying the amount of line out the depth can be altered to suit where the target fish are holding. Saratoga have become a strong drawcard, especially with flyfishers who score with surface and subsurface patterns. Bass respond readily to the same presentations. Cania occasionally produces stud sliver perch. Anglers luck enough to battle one of these 3–4 kg trophy fish are left wondering for a few minutes what in the hell have they hooked.

FACILITIES

There are picnic facilities at the lake but camping isn't permitted. There are two fully contained resorts with cabin accommodations located along the access road into the lake.

BOATING

There are no boating restrictions. A dual lane concrete ramp is serviceable so long as the lake is at least 50 per cent capacity. Alternatively, shore launches are made from a section of hard gravel reached via an adjacent side track.

Cania Dam

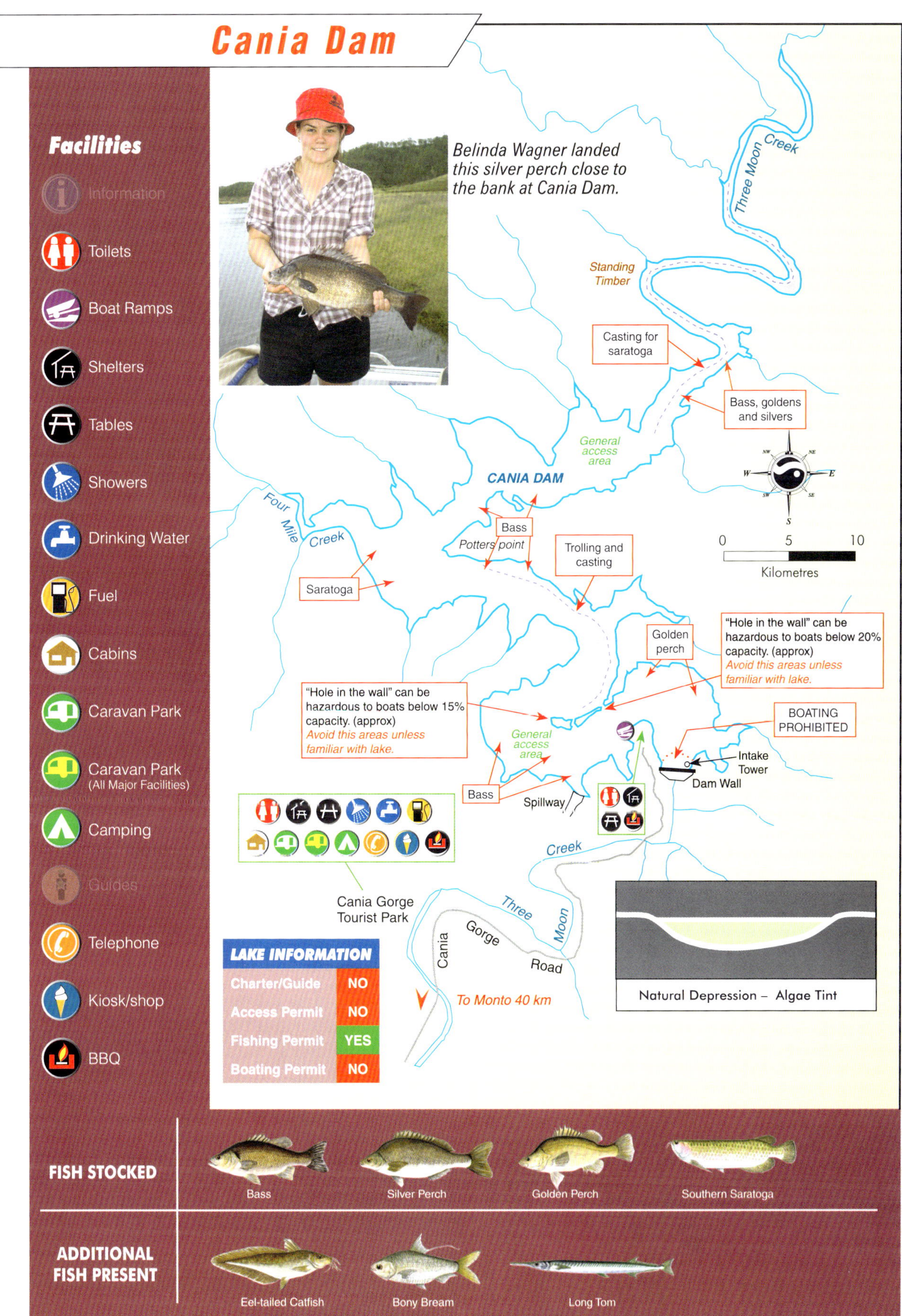

Belinda Wagner landed this silver perch close to the bank at Cania Dam.

LAKE INFORMATION	
Charter/Guide	NO
Access Permit	NO
Fishing Permit	YES
Boating Permit	NO

FISH STOCKED

Bass · Silver Perch · Golden Perch · Southern Saratoga

ADDITIONAL FISH PRESENT

Eel-tailed Catfish · Bony Bream · Long Tom

Chinaman Creek Dam

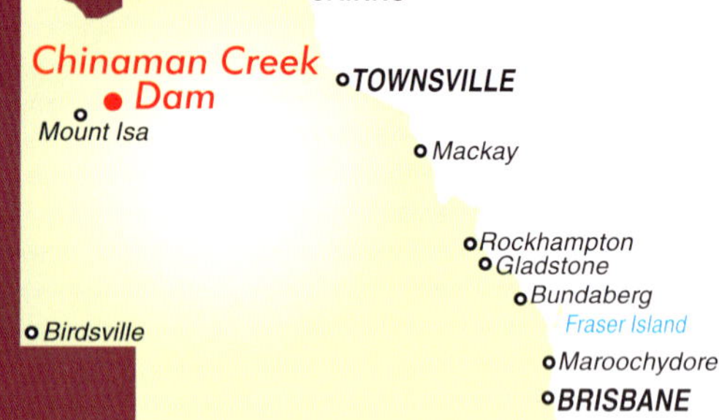

About

Location	Cloncurry
Drainage	Cloncurry River
Surface Area	12 ha
Capacity	650 ML
Usage	Urban Water Supply
Management	Cloncurry Shire Council

Contact for fishing permit: N/A

Red claw is stocked at Chinaman Creek Dam.

Sited 3 km west along the Barkly Highway from the cattle town of Cloncurry—known in laconic gulfspeak as 'the curry'—Chinaman Creek was so-named in the late 1800s when a helter-skelter gold rush brought fortune seekers to those parts from near and far. The Hector Holthouse book River of Gold is compulsory reading for those seeking an accurate historical account of those times. These days Chinaman Creek serves as a domestic water supply for Cloncurry as well as being an important recreational water for those parched parts. For local and traveller alike, this proximity to town makes it easy to duck out for a quick cast.

FISHING (Permit Required)

The progressive Cloncurry Fish Stocking Group has seeded this water with barramundi, sooty grunter, sleepy cod and redclaw. As part of a cluster of stocked lakes around the Cloncurry/Mt. Isa region—those centres lay an hour apart via good road, but watch for stock at night—the Chinaman Creek Dam and other regional stillwaters are well worth including in travel plans. Casting and trolling are both effective and are a matter of personal choice.

FACILITIES

Facilities include shady picnic shelters and barbecue fixtures. Camping is not encouraged.

BOATING

Relaxed regulations allow unrestricted boating and to that end, a concrete ramp has been constructed.

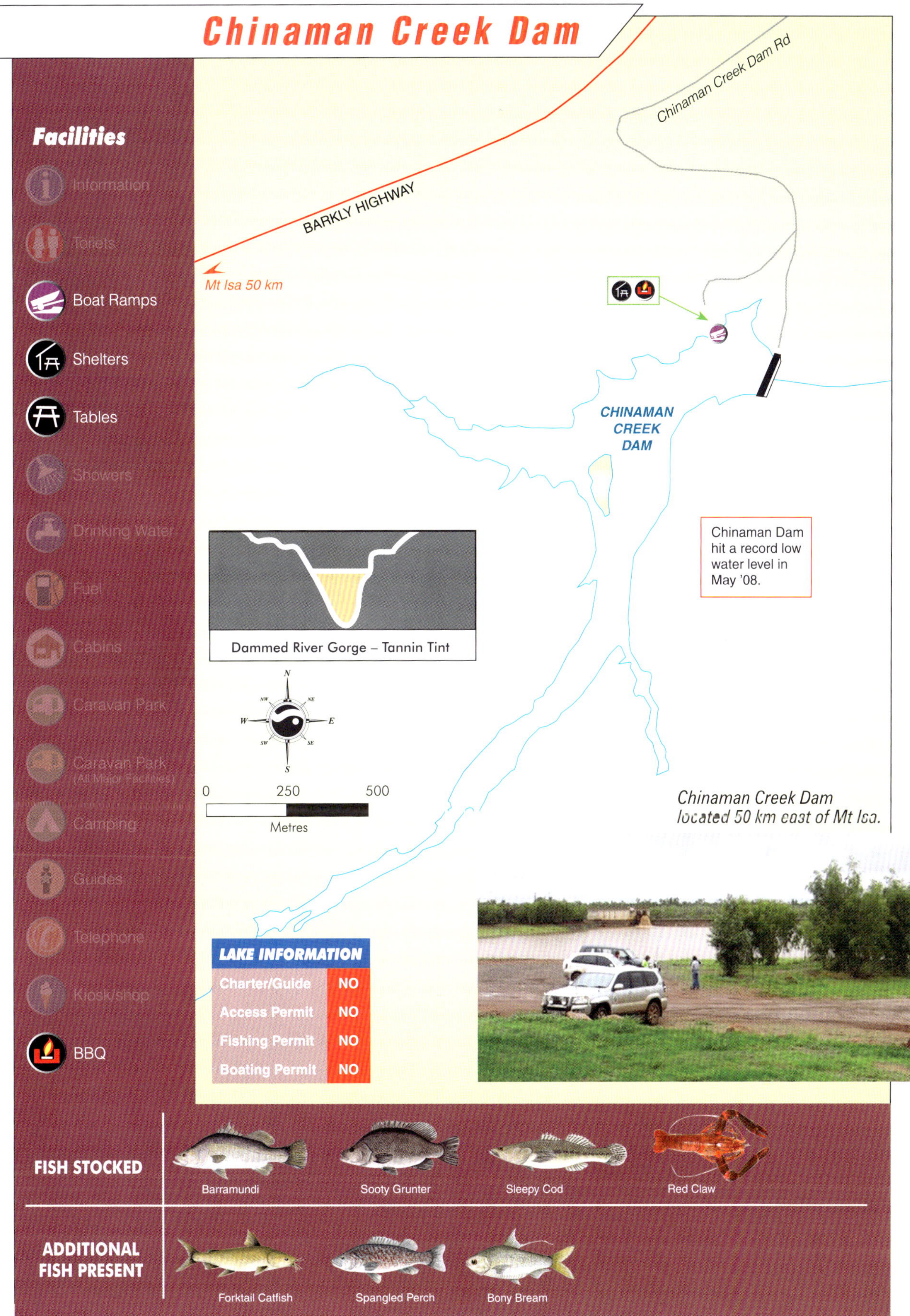
Chinaman Creek Dam
Facilities
Information
Toilets
Boat Ramps
Shelters
Tables
Showers
Drinking Water
Fuel
Cabins
Caravan Park
Caravan Park (All Major Facilities)
Camping
Guides
Telephone
Kiosk/shop
BBQ
Chinaman Creek Dam Rd
BARKLY HIGHWAY
Mt Isa 50 km
CHINAMAN CREEK DAM
Chinaman Dam hit a record low water level in May '08.
Dammed River Gorge – Tannin Tint
N
NE
E
SE
S
SW
W
NW
0
250
500
Metres
Chinaman Creek Dam located 50 km east of Mt Isa.
LAKE INFORMATION
Charter/Guide NO
Access Permit NO
Fishing Permit NO
Boating Permit NO
FISH STOCKED
Barramundi
Sooty Grunter
Sleepy Cod
Red Claw
ADDITIONAL FISH PRESENT
Forktail Catfish
Spangled Perch
Bony Bream

Connolly Dam

About

Location	Warwick
Drainage	Murray-Darling Region
Surface Area	50 ha
Capacity	2,600 ML
Usage	Urban Water
Management	Warwick Shire

Contact for fishing permit: www.smartservice.qld.gov.au

Also known as Silverwood Dam, this is another relatively unknown pocket lake that's been heavily stocked with natives. Located 10 km south of Warwick, off Rosenthal Road, Connolly is certainly worth a cast or two from passing anglers.

FISHING (Permit Required)

Golden perch, silver perch and Murray cod have been stocked to bolster the natural populations of spangled perch and eel-tailed catfish. Golden perch dominate most catches for lure/fly anglers, while silver perch and eel-tailed catfish (dewfish) are more of a baitfishing prospect.

Fishing is restricted to shoreline activity, however access to the water involves some difficulty in reaching, moreso when water levels are high. A section of steep bank to the immediate north of where the vehicle track terminates is worth a few long casts. Lipless crankbaits, spinnerbaits and beetle spins are great lures for exploring Connolly and they have fooled their fair share of cod, yellowbelly and silver perch. Try casting at all the various forms of habitat. Fish won't always be in the most obvious places so be sure to work steep banks, shallow flats, points and the creek bed drop-off.

Paddle craft are permitted but camping is not. Trolling small diving lures is a time and effort efficient way to fish this lake. The extraordinary growth of kayak fishing will open new horizons on small fishy lakes like Connolly. A fishing fact of life for small stillwaters that are lightly fished is the need for a silent approach. Fish become accustomed to boat noise on busy lakes, and that can be enough to quell any strike impulses. Small waters are much easier places for anglers to lose the initiative by announcing themselves.

The exceptionally clear waters of Connolly Dam are another reason for moving slowly and back a little from the bank. Serious anglers can do worse things than study light refraction through water, and gain a working knowledge of fish vision angles. Generally speaking, if you can see fish, they can see you—but not always.

BOATING

No boating is permitted on Connolly Dam except for the use of electric powered boats by local fish stocking group members on Sundays, a ridiculous situation indeed, considering that fish stocking in this dam is funded by the SIP Scheme.

Connolly Dam should be opened to ALL of the public to access or dropped from the SIP scheme.

CAMPING

No camping is permitted at Connolly Dam. Toilets are provided at the lookout adjacent to dam wall.

Connolly Dam

Silverwood Dam

Connolly Dam

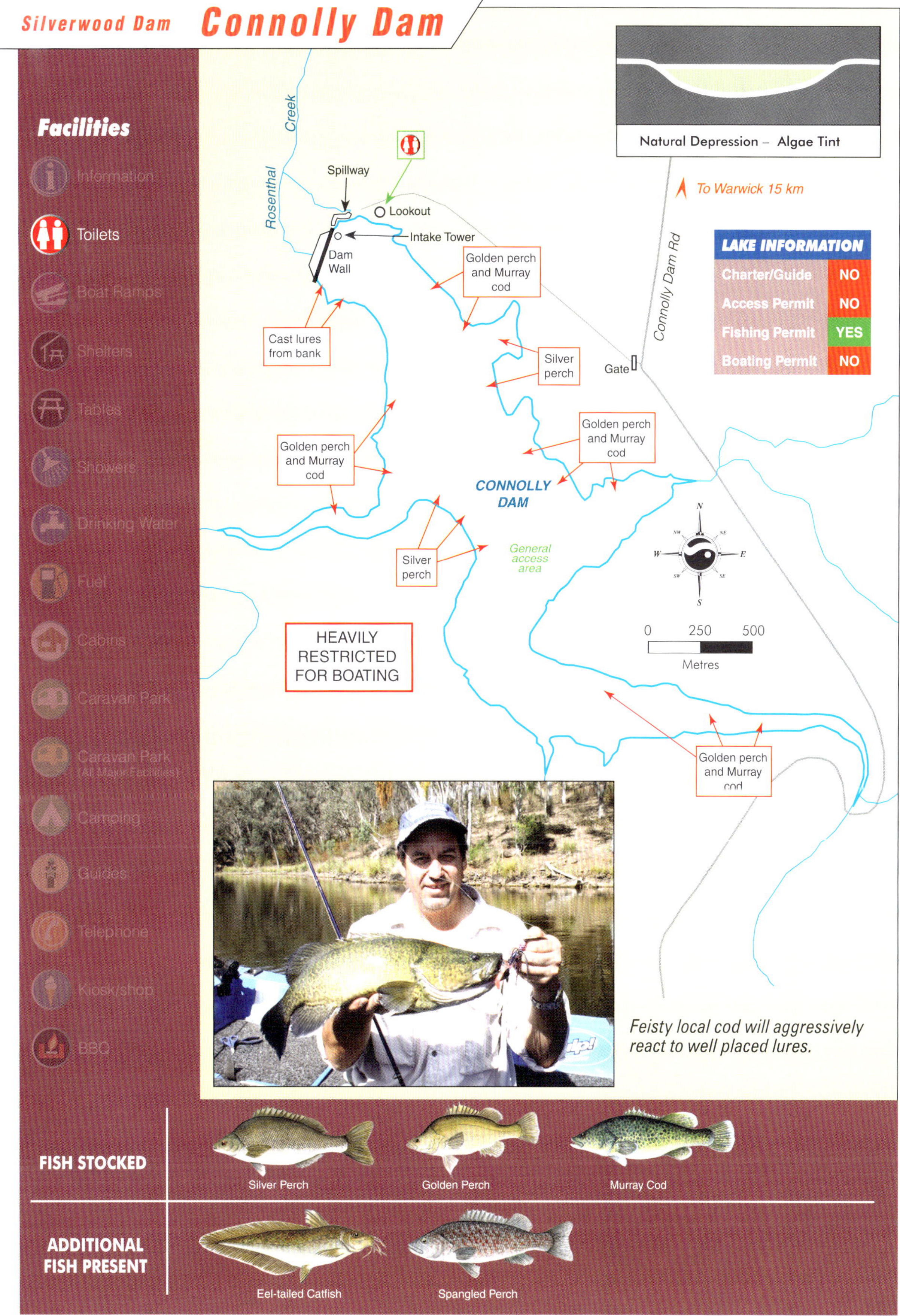

Feisty local cod will aggressively react to well placed lures.

Cooby Dam

About

Location	Toowoomba
Drainage	Codamine River (Hampton)
Surface Area	300 ha
Capacity	23,000 ML
Usage	Domestic
Management	Toowoomba Council

Contact for fishing permit: www.smartservice.qld.gov.au

Built across a Condamine headwater, Cooby Dam is a rather featureless lake has been enhanced by some creative fish habitat erected by the local fish stocking group. Mostly grassy shorelines are shallow and weedy, however the lakebed takes a dished form with the deeper parts in the middle. Various hard objects that attract and hold fish are scattered in the 2–4m depths there. Cooby can develop blue green algae outbreaks than can result in a closure during some summer months.

FISHING (Permit Required)

Cooby is heavily stocked with the three major natives. Trolling is the most widely popular technique. Casting lures to the FADs (fish aggregation devices) is an effective method adopted by those who know their location and can adopt a stealthy approach. Baits are best fished slightly off the bottom using a bubble float. Unfortunately, there are those hogging these limited locations, anchoring boats to preclude others. There are designated 'no go' areas in the extremities of Geham and Cooby creeks and along back from the dam wall.

Small 3 metre divers are suitable for trolling. Golden perch become most active right on dusk and seem to love black and white lures. Slow trolled lipless crankbaits can do the trick and can also be cast closer to the edges where the weed growth permits. Murray cod are not uncommon and are usually caught as bycatch. These fish seem to prefer feeding in the middle of the day. While many trips can fail to produce a cod, it is not uncommon to catch several in a session when they fire up.

FACILITIES

Well maintained day facilities include shelters, barbecues and water. Access is limited to daylight hours and camping is not allowed.

BOATING

Boats are restricted to paddle power and electric outboard. There is a boom gate at the entrance to the lake. The gate requires $2.50 in coins to open so make sure you don't forget your loose change.

Toowoomba City Council 07 4631 6611. Toowoomba District Fish Stocking Assn PO Box 3058 Village Fair Toowoomba Q 4350

Petrol engine restrictions make kayaks the ideal tool to aid anglers target resident fish.

Cooby Dam

LAKE INFORMATION	
Charter/Guide	NO
Access Permit	NO
Fishing Permit	YES
Boating Permit	YES

FISH STOCKED

Silver Perch
Golden Perch
Murray Cod

ADDITIONAL FISH PRESENT

Eel-tailed Catfish
Spangled Perch

Coolmunda Dam

About

Location	Inglewood
Drainage	Murray Darling
Surface Area	1750 ha
Capacity	75,000 ML
Usage	Irrigation/Domestic
Management	Sunwater 07 3884 5317

Contact for fishing permit: www.smartservice.qld.gov.au or Sunwater

Situated 13 km east of Inglewood on the Cunningham Highway lies Coolmunda Dam. Constructed in 1968 for irrigation and town water, the lake has an average depth of 4.3 metres.

FISHING (Permit required)

Thanks to the tireless efforts of the local fish stocking group, Coolmunda is stocked with Murray cod, yellowbelly and silver perch. There are naturally occurring populations of Tandans (eel-tailed catfish) and spangled perch. The recent discovery of European carp in Coolmunda is a concern. One carp was found with a hook through its back, so there is not much doubt about how they arrived.

Coolmunda has two claims to fame. First, it is Queensland's most productive Murray cod lake. That status can be can be attributed to the tireless efforts of the Inglewood Fish Stocking Association who've done a wonderful job in restoring native fish levels in borderland rivers and seeding stillwaters. Though yet to be conformed though scientific sampling, there's every reason to believe that yellowbelly also breed in this shallow and rather snaggy lake.

With greenfish in their sights, the majority of anglers troll at Coolmunda. Their best results come from following the Macintyre Brook bank contours and river bed. Coolmunda fills from that waterway. At peak capacity, those parts along with their plentiful cover lay between 20 and 30 feet below the surface—a depth that's ideal. The back blocks feature thick stands of waist thick timber. Schooling yellowbelly and silver perch are to be found over these flats. Casting spinnerbaits from a drifting boat is productive both in open water and amongst the sticks. Spinnerbaits are less prone to snagging around timber than treble armed lures and are more effective in addressing the water column. Coolmunda is amongst the few lakes where foreshore camping is permitted.

Visitors are requested to leave only footprints, however that's been too much of an ask. The fish Stocking Association members walk the extra mile by cleaning up the mess after busy weekends. Some fisherfolk are grubs.

There is no fishing 200 m upstream and 100 m downstream of the dam wall.

FACILITIES

SunWater Camping Reserve provides free bush camping beside the water. There are cabins and camp sites at the Lake Coolmunda Caravan Park, 07 4652 4171.

Other facilities at the lake include toilets, barbecues, drinking water and telephone.

BOATING

There are no boating restrictions here but caution is advised when travelling around the lake by boat due to the standing timber. There is a concrete boat ramp at the picnic area. There are boats available for hire at the caravan park.

Coolmunda Dam

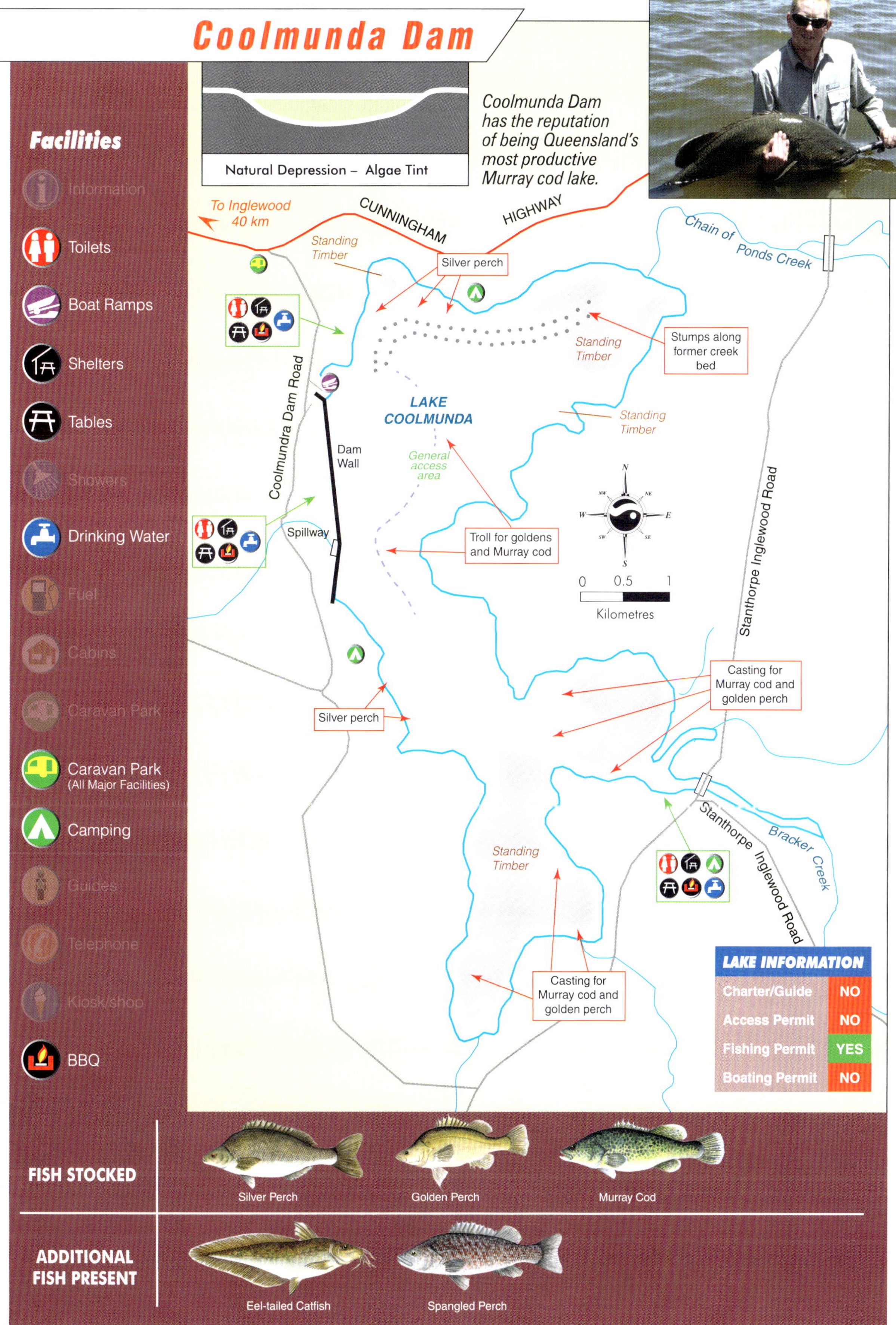
Coolmunda Dam
Facilities
Information
Toilets
Boat Ramps
Shelters
Tables
Showers
Drinking Water
Fuel
Cabins
Caravan Park
Caravan Park
(All Major Facilities)
Camping
Guides
Telephone
Kiosk/shop
BBQ
Natural Depression – Algae Tint
Coolmunda Dam has the reputation of being Queensland's most productive Murray cod lake.
To Inglewood
40 km
CUNNINGHAM
HIGHWAY
Standing Timber
Silver perch
Chain of Ponds Creek
Stumps along former creek bed
Standing Timber
Coolmundra Dam Road
LAKE COOLMUNDA
Standing Timber
Dam Wall
General access area
Spillway
Troll for goldens and Murray cod
N
S
E
W
NW
NE
SW
SE
0
0.5
1
Kilometres
Stanthorpe Inglewood Road
Casting for Murray cod and golden perch
Silver perch
Stanthorpe Inglewood Road
Bracker Creek
Standing Timber
Casting for Murray cod and golden perch
LAKE INFORMATION
Charter/Guide NO
Access Permit NO
Fishing Permit YES
Boating Permit NO
FISH STOCKED
Silver Perch
Golden Perch
Murray Cod
ADDITIONAL FISH PRESENT
Eel-tailed Catfish
Spangled Perch

Corella Park Dam

Weipa
Cooktown
CAIRNS
Corella Park Dam
TOWNSVILLE
Mount Isa
Mackay
Rockhampton
Gladstone
Bundaberg
Fraser Island
Birdsville
Maroochydore
BRISBANE

About

Location	Cloncurry
Drainage	Flinders River
Surface Area	325 ha
Capacity	15,000 ML
Usage	Domestic
Management	Cloncurry Council

Contact for fishing permit: N/A

Corella Dam was constructed in 1959 for town water for Cloncurry. When full it has an average depth of 4.8 metres, however a hole in the dam wall prevents this dam ever being full. This lake is sited on the Corella River about 30 km west of Cloncurry.

FISHING

Fish present are sooty grunter, sleepy cod, striped sleepy cod and redclaw crayfish. The Mt Isa Fish Stocking Group has seeded Corella with sooty grunter to complement an existing sleepy cod population. Sooty grunter have better reputations as fighters than table fish, Their flesh has a leathery texture that finds favour with few. It's a direct contradiction of sorts that the sleepy cod, though a feeble fighter, are (locally) prized as take home fish. Their delicate white flesh is sweet and has a distinctive flavour. Visitor anglers could do worse things than grill a fillet or two over a bed of coals. Red claw crayfish are another 'local' . These tasty natives of the Gulf of Carpentaria drainage system have been released into southern lakes with mixed results. The pattern seems that of boom followed by bust. Redclaw are vegetarian by nature but will invade pots baited with meat or soap. A bait recommended by blokes able to feed a full caravan park is over-ripe mango.

FACILITIES

Camping is permitted below the dam and a motel is available in Cloncurry or Mt Isa. The lake otherwise hosts well maintained picnic facilities.

BOATING

Corella Dam is open to all forms of boating. Boating is permitted on Corella, however there is no ramp and a 4WD could be required for bankside launches.

Corella Park Dam

Corella Park Dam

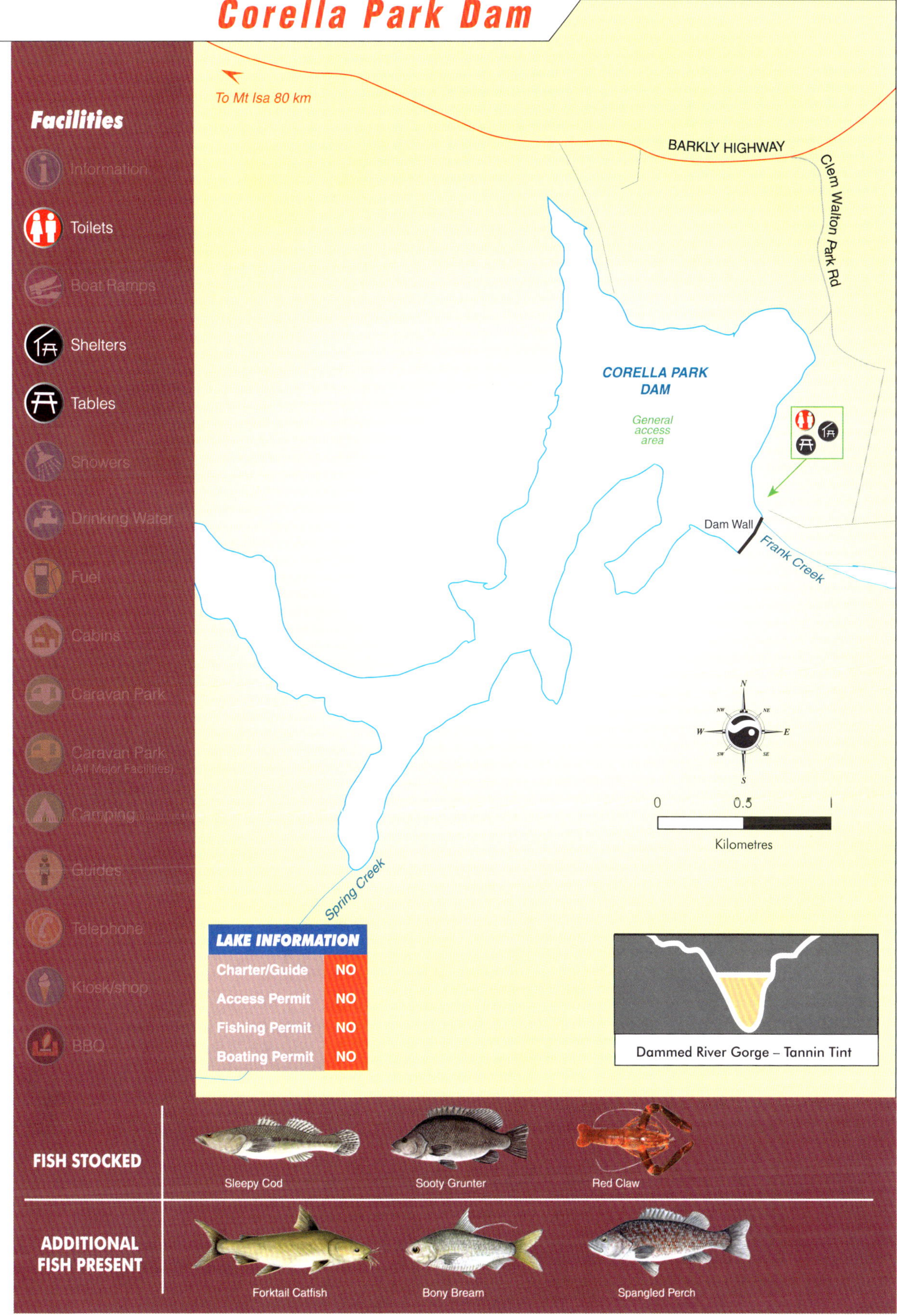

Cressbrook Dam

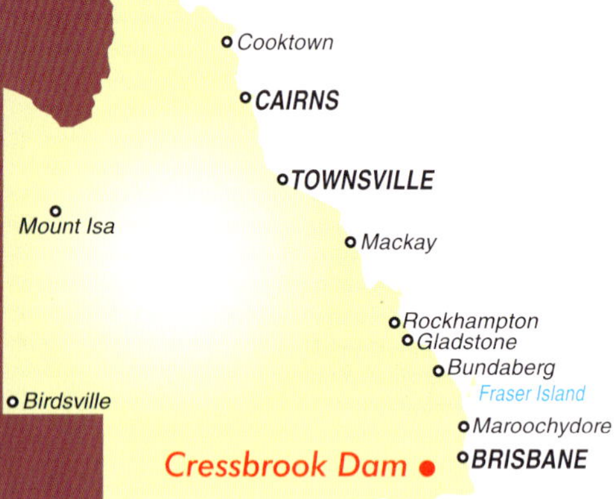

About

Location	Toowoomba
Drainage	Brisbane River System
Surface Area	515 ha
Capacity	81,000 ML
Usage	Irrigation & Urban water
Management	Toowoomba Regional Council 07 4688 6611

Contact for fishing permit: www.smartservice.qld.gov.au or TRC

Constructed in 1983 on an upper Brisbane River feeder, Cressbrook Dam serves as a domestic storage for Toowoomba. But for the efforts of tackle trade identity Peter Taylor and a band of willing helpers this lake may well have remained a locked up sportfish vacuum. Taylor and co. lobbied the city fathers and, subject to conditions, which have been infringement free, received the green light to get a stocking programme underway. Fingerlings were allowed to grow and establish before the lake was opened to the public. When that happened, the results were spectacular.

In years since, stocking densities have as more of less kept pace with the heavy fishing pressures. Fish habitat comprises shallower fringes that have weed cover, and steeper rocky banks.

A beautifully conditioned Cressbrook Dam bass.

FISHING (Permit required)

As with most of Queensland's stocked lakes, Cressbrook produces fish on a year round basis. Throughout the year, bass seem to either favour the deep water or the shallow edges. It seems these fish take up residence in either area as can often be seen by the different colouration. The deeper schools hang around the creek bed in both Cressbrook Creek and Little Oaky Creek (Bull Creek) arms. These fish will take trolled deep diving lures or small shallow running lures fish from a downrigger. Lurecasters can get in to the action with soft plastics, blade baits, ice jigs and deeply presented flies. The edges produce fish year round but it is generally the cooler months which produce the better quality specimens. Surface lures are always the way to start and end the day. During the middle of the day, anglers can experiment with a range of lures as Cressbrook's bass are quite willing to take spinnerbaits, lipless crankbaits, soft plastics, blade baits and suspending jerkbaits. The bass can shut down due to angler pressure so after the action dies down it pays to move on and rest the spot for a few hours.

Snag cover isn't plentiful. On busy weekends, what dead trees there are are usually occupied by boats with baitfishing occupants. Trollers do well working a prominent rock face (typically) known as 'The Bluff' Casting anglers focus on shoreline weedbeds and rocky points. Restricted waters include the water tower and a location known as 'The Gorge' which has been set aside as specific habitat for Mary River cod in the hope a viable stock will establish.

FACILITIES

The Toowoomba City Council maintains well appointed visitor facilities. Rangers and council staff are on site during daylight hours. Limited camping is permitted on a first come best dressed basis, however gates are closed nightly. For bookings, permits and information call Toowoomba City Council 07 4631 6611.

BOATING

At the entrance to the dam, there is a boom gate which requires $2.50 in coins to open. This gate allows access to the boat ramp, playground, barbecues, picnic facilities and campground. An 8 knot speed limit applies. Open Sept/April 6 a.m. to 8 p.m. and May/Aug 7 a.m. to 6 p.m.

Cressbrook Dam

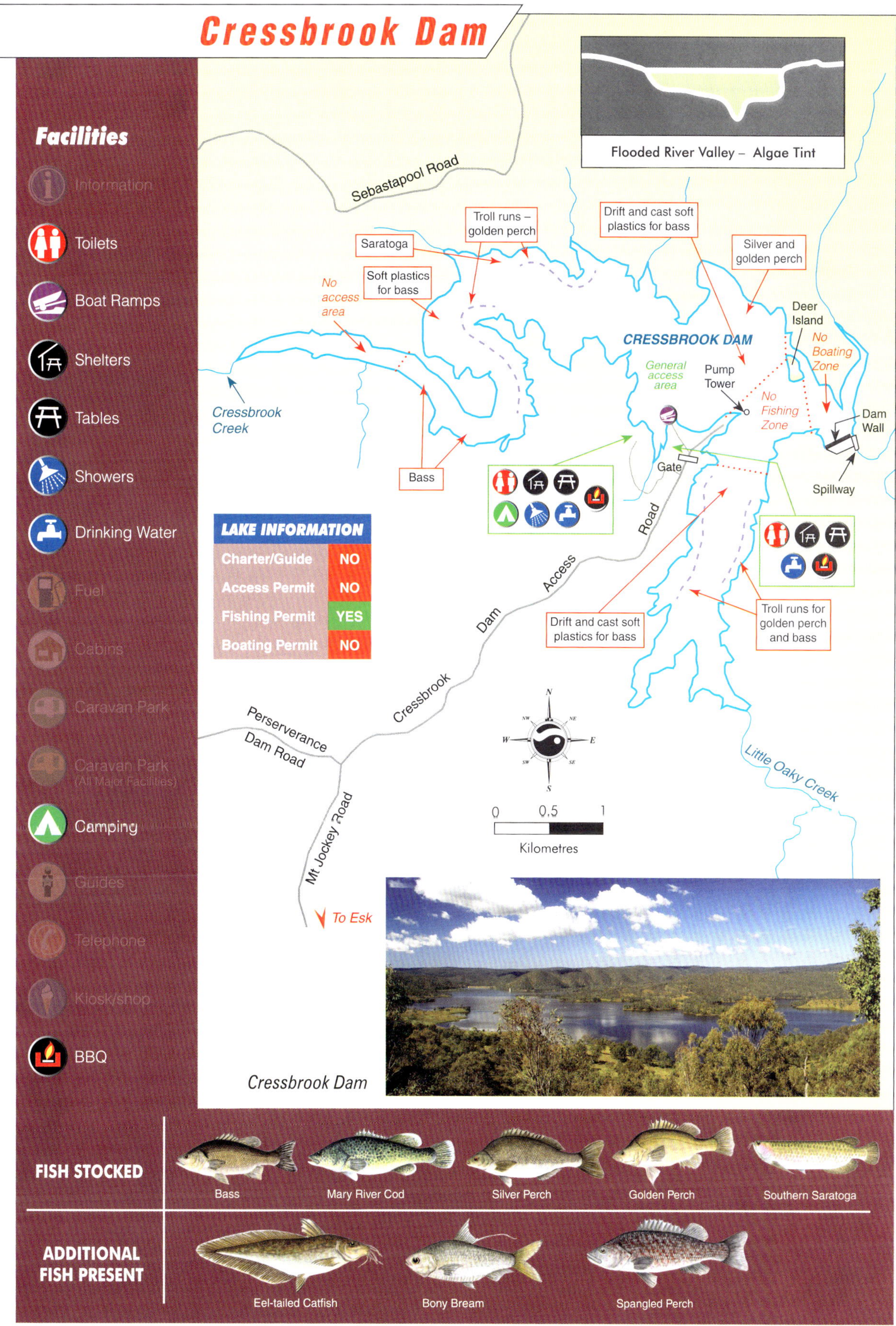

LAKE INFORMATION	
Charter/Guide	NO
Access Permit	NO
Fishing Permit	YES
Boating Permit	NO

Cressbrook Dam

Lake Dalrymple

About

Location	Ravenswood
Drainage	Burdekin River
Surface Area	22,500 ha
Capacity	1,850,000 ML
Usage	Irrigation
Management	Sun Water 07 4783 0555

Contact for fishing permit: www.smartservice.qld.gov.au or Sun Water

Anglers won't be flocking to Queensland's largest impoundment in the same numbers as lesser lakes. Unfortunately, the run-off from the vast Burdekin catchment is coffee coloured and where the various feeders merge to form Dalrymple, those sediments never settle sufficiently for lure fishers to go on the hunt with confidence. If that's not enough, access that involves a 300 km round trip to facilities at the dam wall is a bit of a disincentive.

FISHING (Permit required)

There are various access points on the four main arms extending from the main basin but these require local knowledge and the consent of property owners. The lack of clarity hides numerous rock spires, ridges and hillets rising from the lake floor. One speeds across those waters at considerable peril.

Fish found in Lake Dalrymple include eels, archer fish, sooty grunter, sleepy cod, longtom, leathery grunter, golden perch, silver perch, eel-tailed catfish, forktail catfish and barramundi. Only barramundi are stocked regularly, the remainder have self-sustaining populations. There are also redclaw crayfish present.

Explorations are painfully slow. To prove the point that barra, sooty grunter and sleepy cod can be taken on lures in this intimidating lake and a few adventurous anglers have done so—but only after many casts.

There are yellowbelly in the Belyando arm that probably move down into the lake. How they got there, no one knows. Perhaps they were translocated at some stage, perhaps they are part of a natural stock as are the fish in the Fitzroy. Torrential summer rains though February '08 saw two metres of water pouring over the spillway for days on end. It is probable that the barramundi stock would have evacuated the lake. These circumstances may see Dalrymple remain a low stocking priority.

Be aware that the lake is a natural habitat for the saltwater crocodile, so beware.

FACILITIES

Adjacent to the lake is the Burdekin Dam Holiday Park, 07 4770 3178 or 1800 673 688, which has powered sites, camp sites and motel style units. At the lake there are numerous facilities including picnic grounds, barbecues, water, telephone and kiosk.

BOATING

No restrictions apply and it is open to all boating activities. There is a single lane concrete boat ramp.

Sooties and catfish from the upper Burdekin river.

Sooties hit soft plastics hard in Burdekin Falls Dam.

Lake Dyer

About

Location	Laidley
Drainage	Greater Brisbane System
Surface Area	100 ha
Capacity	6950 ML
Usage	Irrigation
Management	Sun Water 07 3884 5317

Contact for fishing permit: www.smartservice.qld.gov.au or Sun Water

Also called Bill Gunn Dam after the National Party politician, Lake Dyer is one of a number of small, relatively shallow and heavily used storages in the fertile Lockyer Valley. This southern sidearm of the much bigger Brisbane Valley is a food basket where extensive vegetable and cereal crops are grown. An offstream storage that's filled from Laidley Creek (an upper reach of the Brisbane River) Lake Dyer is subject to high drawdowns and summer evaporation. A significant blue/green algae problem develops during summer, a consequence of the abundant spread of phosphate fertilisers. Besides health hazards, well signposted on waters where outbreaks occur, departmental advice is that fish from those lakes not be consumed. The parasitic sores evident on native fish from poor water quality should be a veritable red light.

FISHING (Permit Required)

Despite fluctuations and marginal water quality, this lake fishes well. The up/down water level helps control weed growths, if not the algae. This provides a bankside option. It's not uncommon to see locals casting from the shore on warm afternoons. A lack of structure favours covering water either by trolling or fanning out casts. Small diving lures and spinnerbaits work well.

After the 2011 floods, many big golden perch and bass were rescued and placed back in the dam. There will be a distinct size difference between these older fish and the newly stocked ones for some years to come.

The local fish stocking group is the Lockyer Valley Fish Restocking and Management Assn, 2 Alexander St, Laidley, Qld, 4341.

FACILITIES

Camping sites and powered caravan sites are situated on the lake shore at the council run caravan park, along with toilets, showers, barbecues, drinking water and picnic tables. Gates are closed overnight. Caretaker contact 07 5465 3698.

BOATING

There are no boating restrictions on Lake Dyer, however there is a maximum of eight boats allowed on the lake at any time. A single lane concrete ramp is provided for launching when the lake is full. When low, it is a matter of launching off the firm bank in front if the camping area.

Almost! This silver perch couldn't quite get the lure down.

Bill Gunn Dam

Lake Dyer

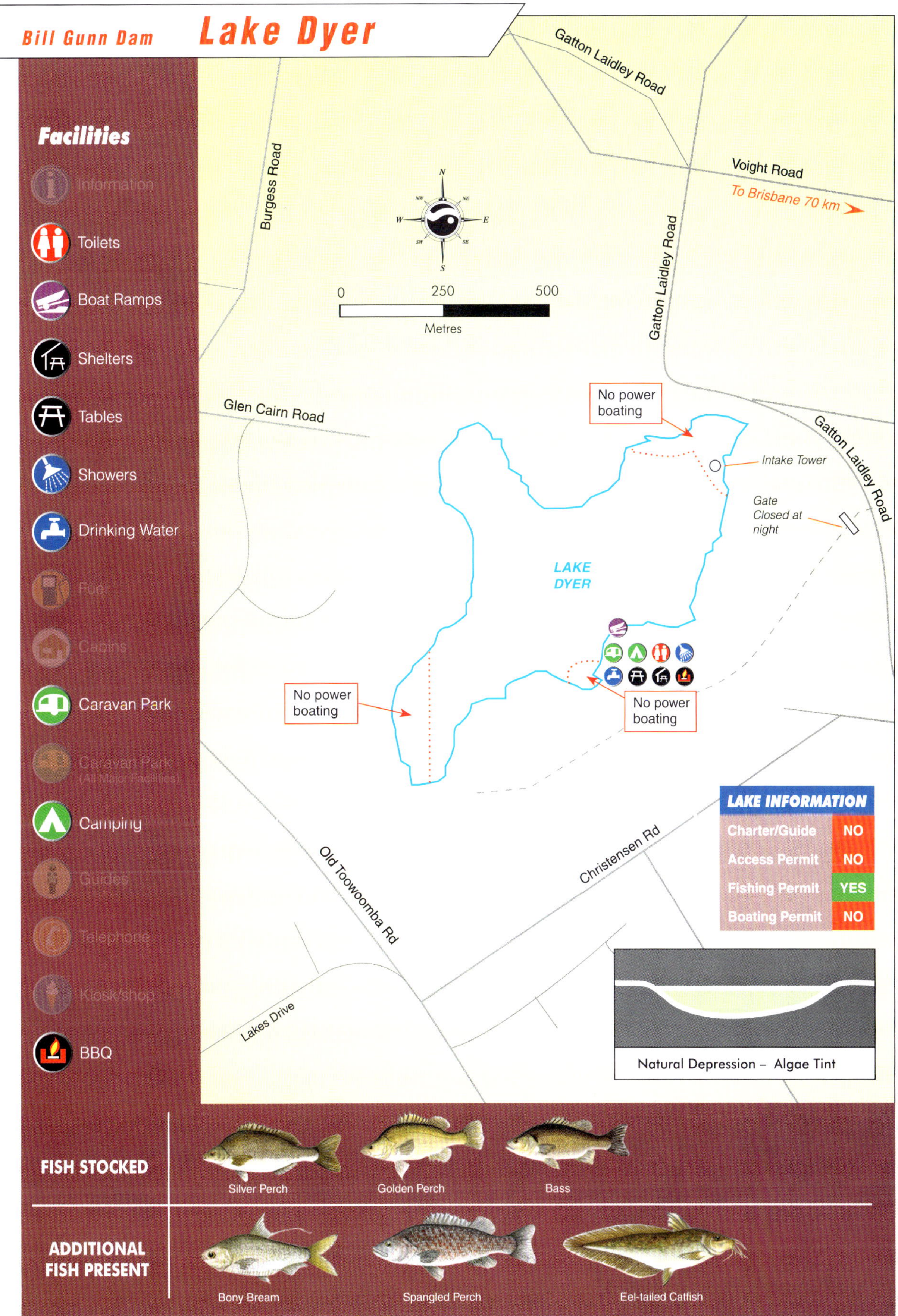

LAKE INFORMATION	
Charter/Guide	NO
Access Permit	NO
Fishing Permit	YES
Boating Permit	NO

FISH STOCKED

Silver Perch
Golden Perch
Bass

ADDITIONAL FISH PRESENT

Bony Bream
Spangled Perch
Eel-tailed Catfish

East Leichhardt Dam

About

Location	Mt Isa
Drainage	Leichhardt River
Surface Area	150 ha
Capacity	12,000 ML
Usage	Irrigation
Management	Sun Water 07 4052 3434

Contact for fishing permit: Sun Water

East Leichardt Dam was built in 1961 to supply the township of the now closed Mary Kathleen Uranium Mine. It has an average depth of 8.1 metres.

Also called Lake Mary Kathleen after the Mt. Isa outpost mining town, this little lake is the uppermost to be built along the rocky Leichhardt River system. Moondarra and Julius lay downstream.

FISHING

Another veritable oasis, the East Leichhardt Dam was completed in 1961 and in years since has been stocked with barramundi. These complement existing populations of sooty grunter, sleepy cod, archer fish, alligator gar (longtom) and redclaw. A little out of the way for the family sedan, access calls for a 4WD. The East Leichhardt Dam is open to power boats but launching is via an earthen ramp.

This attractive lake is yet another that calls for stealth. The tendency for barra to become boat shy has already been mentioned. To that it should be added that sooty grunter can be more alert than gun shy brown trout. Another item that can be safely added to the 'silent running' routine is to turn off sonars whenever fishing from stationary boats—and when in shallow water. There is no doubt that barramundi feel the tick-tick signal pulse, especially when inside the unit's footprint. When pinged, the instincts of lake fish become more focused on moving than snapping at any lure that may suddenly appear. The camping facilities amid attractive surrounds are well kept secrets.

CAMPING

Camping is permitted at East Leichhardt Dam, however there are no facilities provided. Other accommodation is provided in Mt Isa.

BOATING

It is open to all forms of boating, no restrictions apply. There is no concrete boat ramp, however boats can be launched with care from gravel ramp.

Sooty grunters have no respect for size when it comes to attacking lures.

Lake Mary Kathleen

East Leichhardt Dam

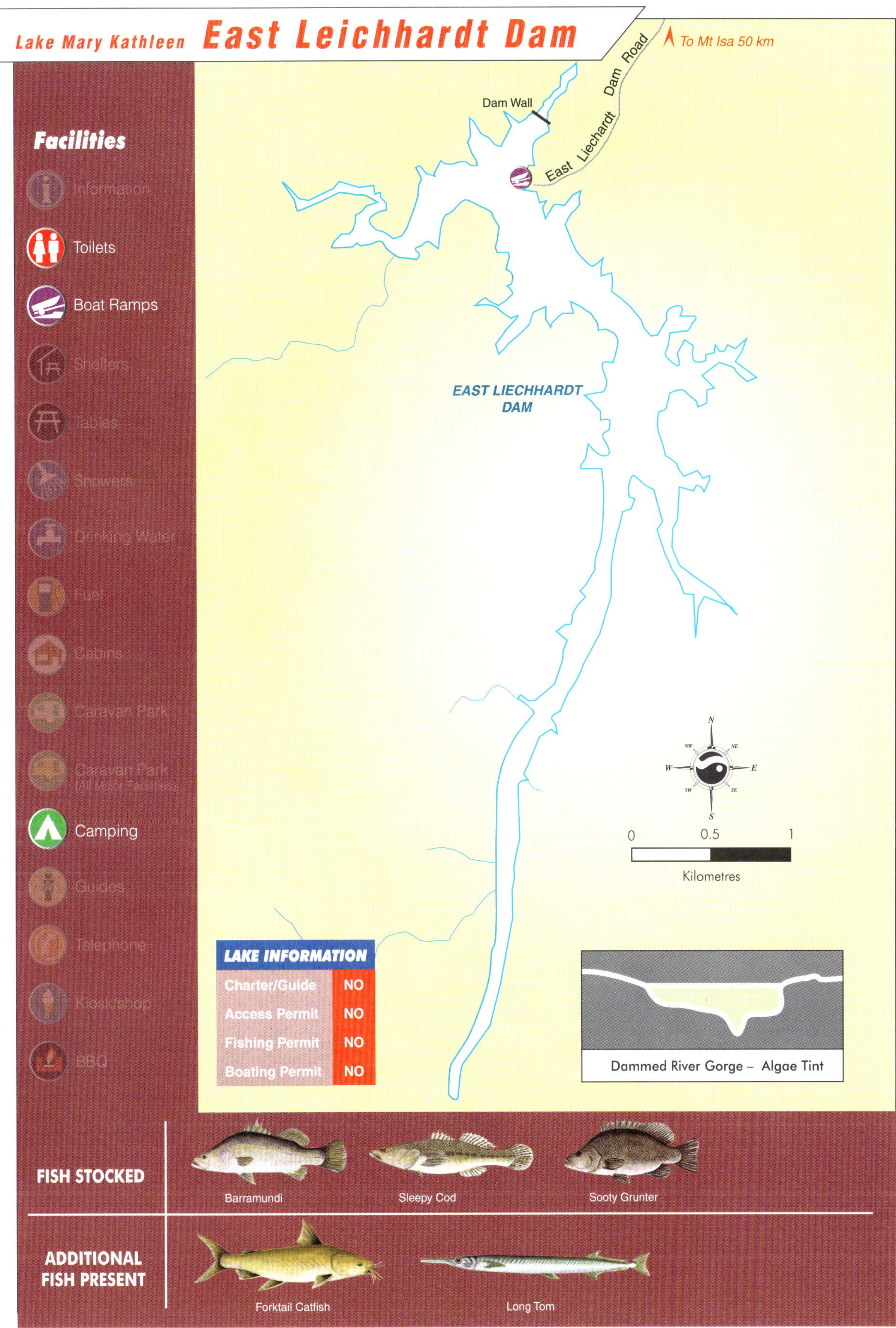

LAKE INFORMATION	
Charter/Guide	NO
Access Permit	NO
Fishing Permit	NO
Boating Permit	NO

Eungella Dam

Weipa
Cooktown
CAIRNS
TOWNSVILLE
Mount Isa
Eungella Dam
Mackay
Rockhampton
Gladstone
Bundaberg
Fraser Island
Birdsville
Maroochydore
BRISBANE

About

Location	Mackay
Drainage	Pioneer River / Broken System
Surface Area	900 ha
Capacity	130,000 ML
Usage	Irrigation & Power Generation
Management	Sun Water 07 4783 0555

Contact for fishing permit: www.smartservice.qld.gov.au or Sun Water

Another 'high country' lake, Eungella sits on a steep high escarpment a two hour drive to the west of Mackay. Barra have been stocked but not with the success of sooty grunter. One of Queensland's more established freshwater fisheries, Eungella has made a name for producing extra oversized sooty grunter and more recently barramundi.

FISHING (Permit Required)

Eungella Dam is stocked with sooty grunter, saratoga, sleepy cod and barramundi. The local stocking group, Mackay Area Fish Stocking Association (MAFSA), are one of Queensland's most proactive groups. MAFSA runs its own fish hatchery breeding sooty grunter to be stocked into Eungella, Kinchant and Teemburra dams.

Given the relatively small size of this dam, the extent of the angler effort and a geography that stacks the odds on ideal fishing weather, Eungella can be safely pigeon holed as a low yield barra lake. The water is characterised by a cleared area adjacent to the wall. This forms a basin of sorts. Much of the remaining lake is studded with standing dead timber. The sprawling branches make ideal fish cover.

Thumping sooties to 6 kg aren't uncommon in that territory as are accounts of busted lures and broken lines. If stud sooties are on the hit list, Eungella is the place, but long accurate casts amongst the timber are essential. The difficulty compounds when using braids and winds are swirling. The best lures for the situation are spinnerbaits and jighead/soft plastic combinations. It is important to have reels engaged as lures splash down—sooties are hot on the drop. Some almighty backlashes happen to those who aren't ready. A hard drag setting is another piece of forward planning. Sooties bear down and can test fibre and sinew.

Local sooty grunter are territorial and aggressive towards vibrating and noisy lure types.

FACILITIES

Bush camping is allowed with toilets, cold showers, barbecues, picnic tables and play ground provided. Accommodation is available 25 km away at Enugella Holiday Park 07 4958 4590

BOATING

There are no boating restrictions here, however no boat ramps are provided. Smaller boats can be launched at one of the designated areas.

Eungella Dam

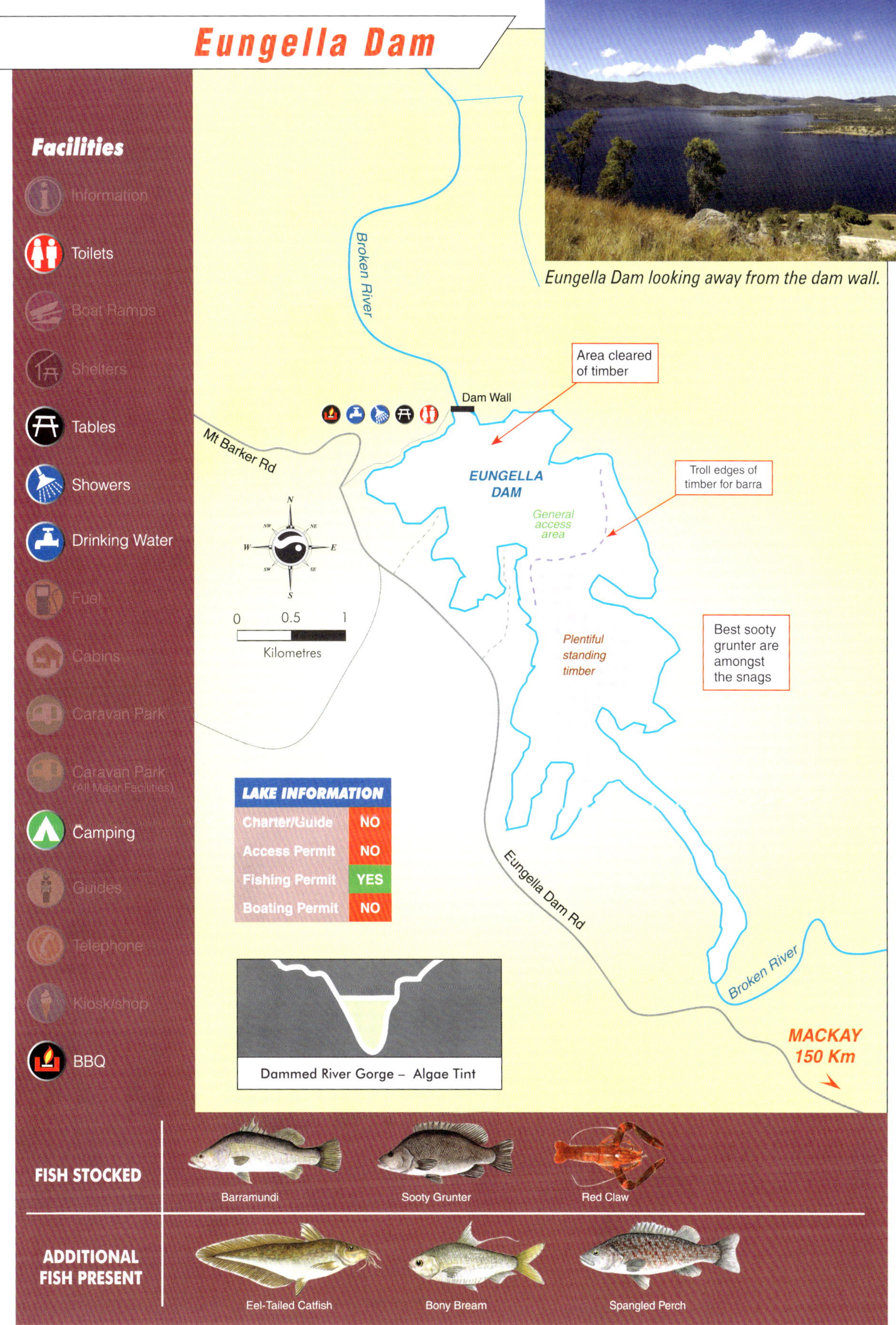

Eungella Dam looking away from the dam wall.

LAKE INFORMATION	
Charter/Guide	NO
Access Permit	NO
Fishing Permit	YES
Boating Permit	NO

Ewen Maddock Dam

About

Location	Mooloolah
Drainage	Addington Creek
Surface Area	375 ha
Capacity	16,500 ML
Usage	Domestic supply
Management	South East Queensland Water

Contact for fishing permit: Caloundra City Council

One of many smaller stocked stillwaters, Ewen Maddock was built in 1973 on Addington Creek, a tributary of the Mooloolah River. Supplying domestic waters for the Sunshine Coast, it is a generally shallow and weedy lake that will test casting anglers. Deep waters are pretty much limited to the area immediately behind the dam wall.

FISHING

Though stocked with bass, golden and silver perch, a combination of weedy edges and boat restrictions along with a daylight hours only fishing window keeps the casual angler away. Boomer bass are a result, but not without considerable effort. Noted fishing guide Paul Dolan did time on the fish stocking association and had the foresight to seed saratoga. This lake is better suited to specialist anglers willing to shed a bucket of sweat for a shot at big bass or stud 'toga. A small cadre of flyfishers who've perfected weedless presentations fish the lake in kayaks very successfully.

The local fish stocking group is the Ewen Maddock Dam Fishing & Stocking Association, PO Box 115 Caloundra, Qld, 4551.

FACILITIES

Ewen Maddock has day facilities for visitors. Camping is not permitted, nor is access between dusk and dawn. However, there is a group camping site on the eastern side of the lake.

BOATING

Boats are limited to paddle power. The restrictions on prop driven vessels is on account of noxious aquatic weed and the fear that the agitation from propellers will break off parts of these plants and aid its spread. Further enquiries Caloundra City Council 07 5491 0200.

Paddle power is the only option on Ewen Maddock Dam making float tubes and kayaks ideal.

Ewen Maddock Dam

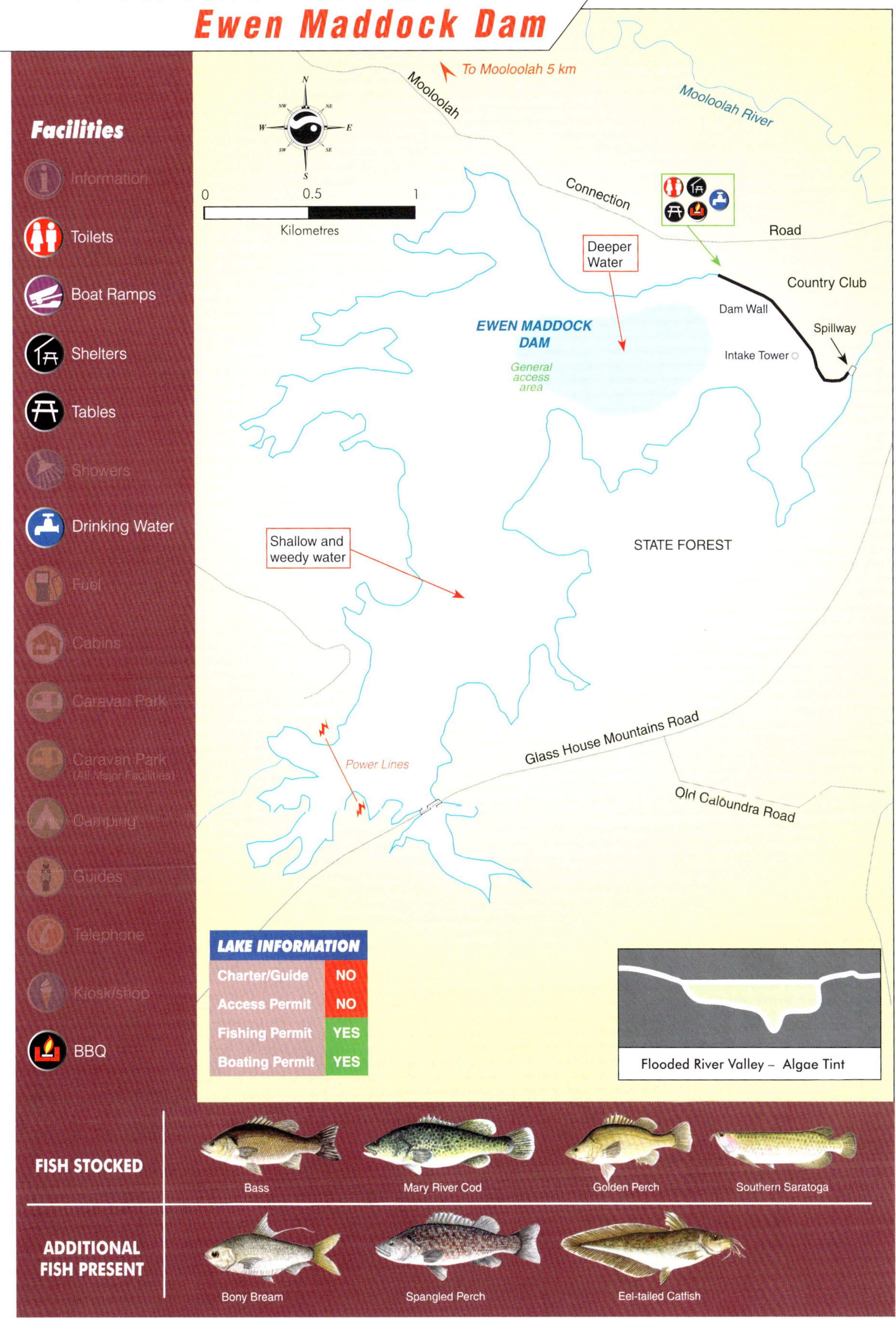

Fairbairn Dam

Weipa
Cooktown
CAIRNS
TOWNSVILLE
Mount Isa
Mackay
Fairbairn Dam
Rockhampton
Gladstone
Bundaberg
Fraser Island
Birdsville
Maroochydore
BRISBANE

About

Location	Emerald
Drainage	Fitzroy
Surface Area	18,000 ha
Capacity	1,300,000 ML
Usage	Irrigation
Management	Sun Water 07 4992 8111

Contact for fishing permit: Sun Water

Fairbairn is one of the states largest dams. Also called Lake Maraboon (means 'where the black duck flies'), Fairbairn Dam covers a vast and relatively shallow basin. The main fish habitat is standing (and fallen) timber. In places, the timber density can be disorienting. When the lake is full, navigable waters extend for over 40 km up the Nogoa River.

FISHING

A famed upstream yellowbelly spawning run occurs during a big rise. An enormous bony bream biomass provides huge angling potential. Western rivers strain Murray cod were stocked during the 1980s and have established into a breeding population. In more recent years, limited numbers of barramundi were released. These rapidly matured, with fish to 140 cm being taken by anglers fishing from the bank. The rocky foreshores adjacent to the dam wall that extend beyond a bouldered point to a boat launching area are the best places to try for barra and cod.

The barramundi status remains uncertain following heavy rains that over two metres of water pouring over the spillway. It's a consolation of sorts that evacuations generally mean more fish in the river below. An unfortunate consequence of big rains is marginal water clarity. The lake can take several years to clear sufficiently for one to fish confidently with lures. Maraboon is a redclaw Mecca. More combined effort goes into their pursuit than that currently expended on finned fish.

Barra have been stocked in the river below the dam and saratoga (to 5 kg) in the lake proper. There is a ban on fishing within 200 metres from the dam wall, below the dam the ban extends to 400 metres.

FACILITIES

The Lake Maraboon Holiday Village, 07 4982 3677, on the water's edge provides caravan and tent sites as well as cabins and villas. Other facilities include toilets, showers, barbecues, picnic areas, drinking water, telephone, restaurant and petrol.

BOATING

There are no restrictions and there is a concrete launching ramp.

Fairbairn Dam

(Lake Maraboon) Fairbairn Dam

Facilities

- Information
- Toilets
- Boat Ramps
- Shelters
- Tables
- Showers
- Drinking Water
- Fuel
- Cabins
- Caravan Park
- Caravan Park (All Major Facilities)
- Camping
- Guides
- Telephone
- Kiosk/shop
- BBQ

To Emerald 30 km
Capricorn Highway
Denison Road
N
S
E
W
NW
NE
SW
SE
0
2.5
5
Kilometres
Restricted area
Lake Maraboon Holiday Village
Spillway
Fairbairn Dam Road
Dense standing timber
Retaining Wall
FAIRBAIRN DAM
Rocky shoreline
General access area
Kangaroo Island
Jig blades and rattlers for goldens
Troll close to shore for cod
Gregory Highway

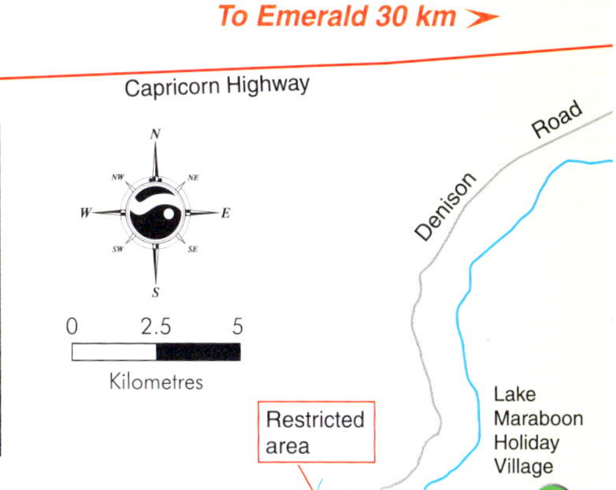

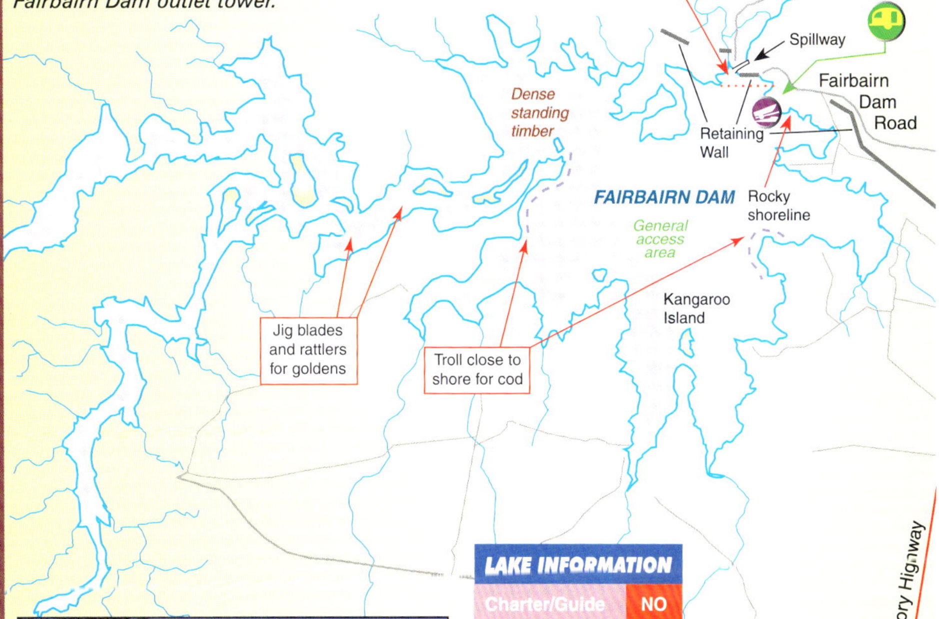

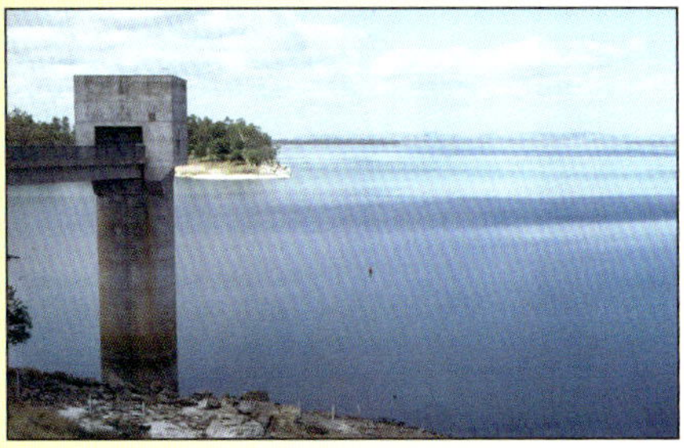

Fairbairn Dam outlet tower.

LAKE INFORMATION	
Charter/Guide	NO
Access Permit	NO
Fishing Permit	YES
Boating Permit	NO

Fishy rock formation at Fairbairn Dam.

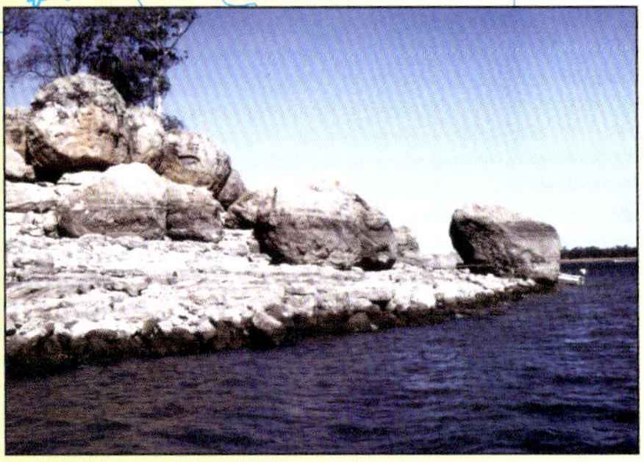

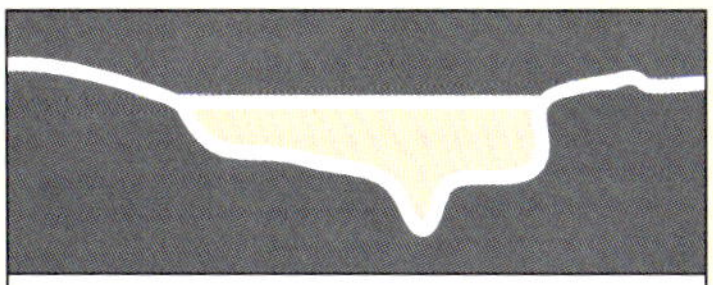

Flooded River Valley – Milky

FISH STOCKED

Barramundi, Murray Cod, Southern Saratoga, Silver Perch

ADDITIONAL FISH PRESENT

Eel-tailed Catfish, Spangled Perch, Red Claw, Sooty Grunter, Golden Perch

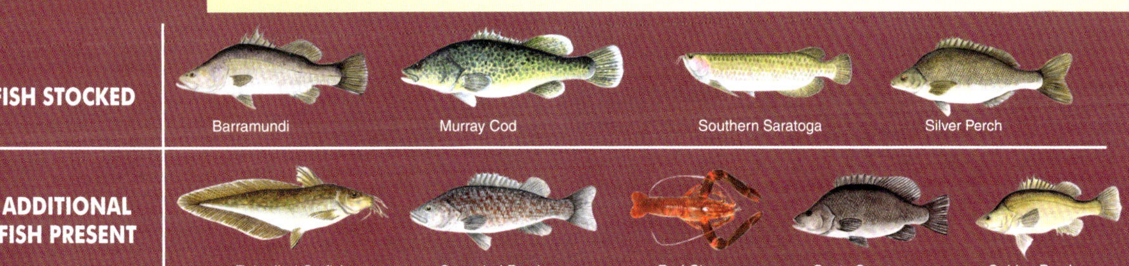

Glenlyon Lake

Weipa
Cooktown
CAIRNS
TOWNSVILLE
Mount Isa
Mackay
Rockhampton
Gladstone
Bundaberg
Fraser Island
Birdsville
Maroochydore
BRISBANE
Glenlyon Lake

About

Location	Texas
Drainage	Murray Darling
Surface Area	1800 ha
Capacity	254,000 ML
Usage	Irrigation & Town Water
Management	Sun Water 07 3884 5317

Contact for fishing permit: www.smartservice.qld.gov.au or Sun Water

Being one of Queensland's better known freshwater destinations, Glenlyon Dam is a moderate sized lake with an average depth of 4.3 metres. It is also called Pike Creek Dam or Pike Creek Reservoir.

Completed on a Dumaresq River feeder in 1976, Glenlyon was the first Queensland lake to be stocked with native fish, especially Murray cod. New South Wales Fisheries were quietly seeding this borderland lake with their excess native fish fingerlings as anglers from the southern State were fishing there. The bananabender hierarchy hit the roof when they found out. These days, stocking is in the hands of people who see the big picture.

FISHING (Permit Required)

Golden perch dominate catches here, but it is the chance of tangling with a big Murray cod that has put Glenlyon on the map. Silver perch are also stocked and there is an endemic population of Tandans (eel-tailed catfish) and spangled perch.

Glenlyon is rich in fish habitat. There are numbers of the rocky points that Murray cod favour, along with sprawling ironbark snags. An area known as the Limestone Caves, midway along the main arm, holds yellowbelly schools. When the lake it at low levels, the chalk like boulders comprising the formation are exposed. Trolling cover along the lake fringes is a popular and effective. Lure makers Peter Newell and Trevor McFeeters drew on Glenlyon experiences when designing famed patterns like the Kadaitcha and Tenterfield Shrimp. Bobbing around dead trees with shrimp and crayfish accounts from most of the weighty yellowbelly bags.

Glenlyon is subject to seasonal convection currents that bring about a lake 'roll over'. The process may take a week but sees fish elsewhere as the roiled and deoxygenated water from the lake bed takes over the surface layer.

FACILITIES

The Glenlyon Dam Tourist Park, 02 6737 5266, features cabins, powered or unpowered sites and kiosk. Facilities include drinking water, boat hire, public phones, tennis court, ice, gas and petrol, and food.

BOATING

There are no boating restrictions here except for the restricted area near the dam wall.

Note: use caution when navigating this lake as there are large areas of standing timber and submerged logs, particularly in the upper reaches of feeder creeks.

A low Glenlyon Lake.

Glenlyon Lake

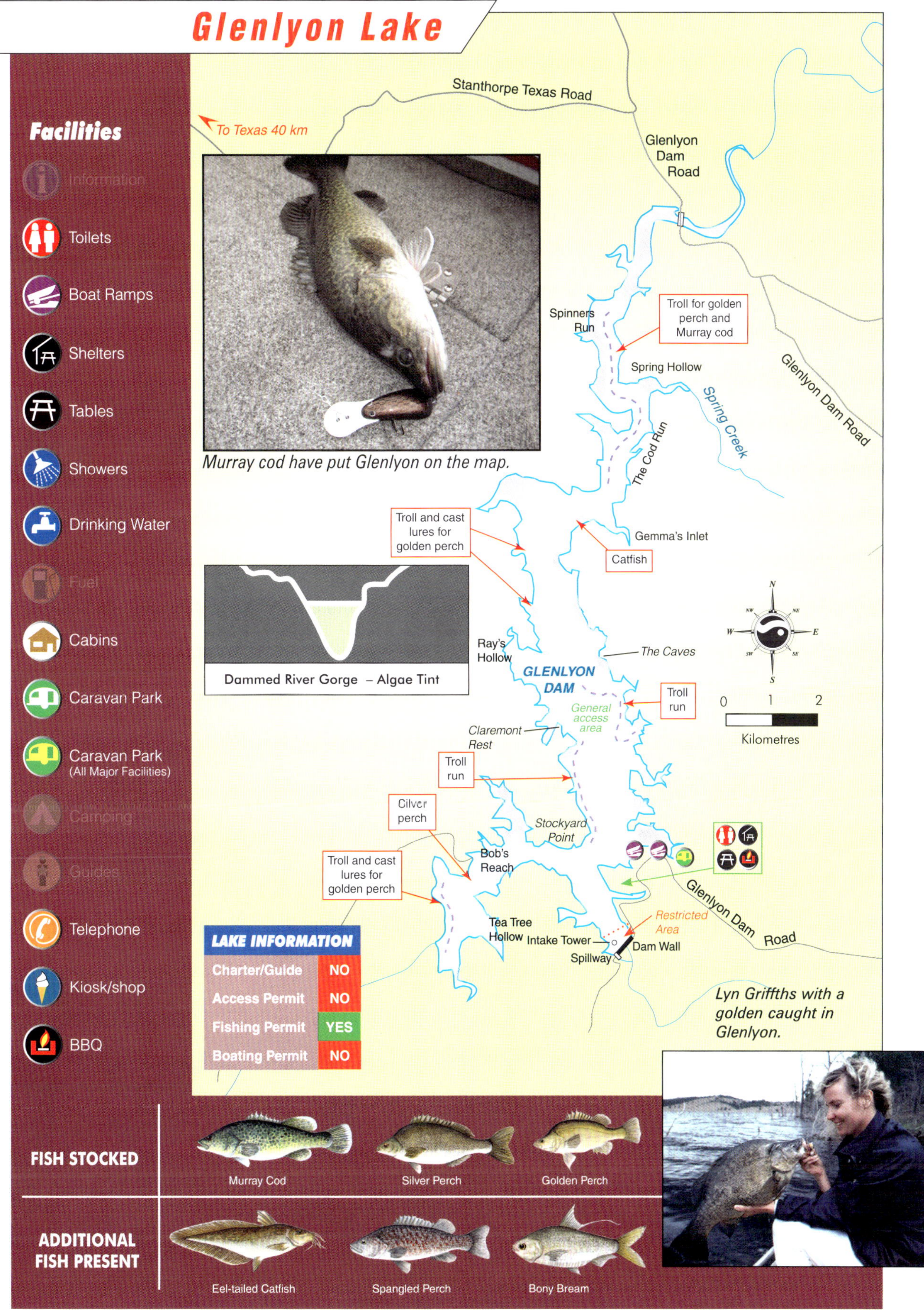

Murray cod have put Glenlyon on the map.

Lyn Griffths with a golden caught in Glenlyon.

Lake Julius

About

Location	Mt Isa
Drainage	Leichhardt
Surface Area	1425 ha
Capacity	127,000 ML
Usage	Irrigation & Town Water
Management	Mount Isa City Council 07 4095 8323

Contact for fishing permit: N/A

This outback oasis was completed in 1976 and is reached via a hundred kilometres of mostly bad road from the Barkley Highway. However, the bone jarring and axle snapping washouts can be worth the trip.

Julius is a bird paradise. Of orno-interest might be the fact that Australia's rarest raptors—the red goshawk and grey falcon—have been spotted there. Sure footed lotus birds that scamper across the water lilies are common and approachable.

FISHING

Lake Julius is well known locally as an excellent sooty grunter fishery. Sooty grunter were so well stocked that they have established into a breeding population and hence is the primary source of sooty brood stock for the Mount Isa Fish Stocking Group (MIFSG) breeding program.

Julius has more recently been seeded with barramundi and saratoga. Other naturally occurring residents include redclaw, sleepy cod, archer fish forktail and eel-tail catfish and freshwater long-toms as thick as a dairy farmer's forearms. Freshwater crocodiles are also plentiful and represent little danger. Shoreline cover that includes rock bluffs, snags and lily pad expanses makes fishing a veritable lottery—one doesn't know what will strike next.

A combination of factors will ensure high quality fishing into the future. Julius remains lightly fished. The solid two plus hour drive from Mt. Isa is a bit much for locals considering that Lake Moondarra is much closer to town and more heavily stocked with barramundi. But for travellers with time and the wheels, Julius is a stopover that can rate amongst the highlights of any black stump angling adventure.

FACILITIES

There is no camping at the lake. Facilities include picnic tables, barbecues and drinking water. It had a kiosk and, just downstream of the dam wall, the Lake Julius Recreational Camp, 07 4742 5998, that had cabins, caravan and tent sites. Unfortunately, these facilities are not operating at this writing. Sunwater may reopen or contract their operation at some time in the future

BOATING

There are no restrictions and there is a single lane boat ramp.

A fishing oasis in the harsh outback near Mt Isa, Lake Julius has excellent Sooty Grunter fishing on offer.

Lake Julius

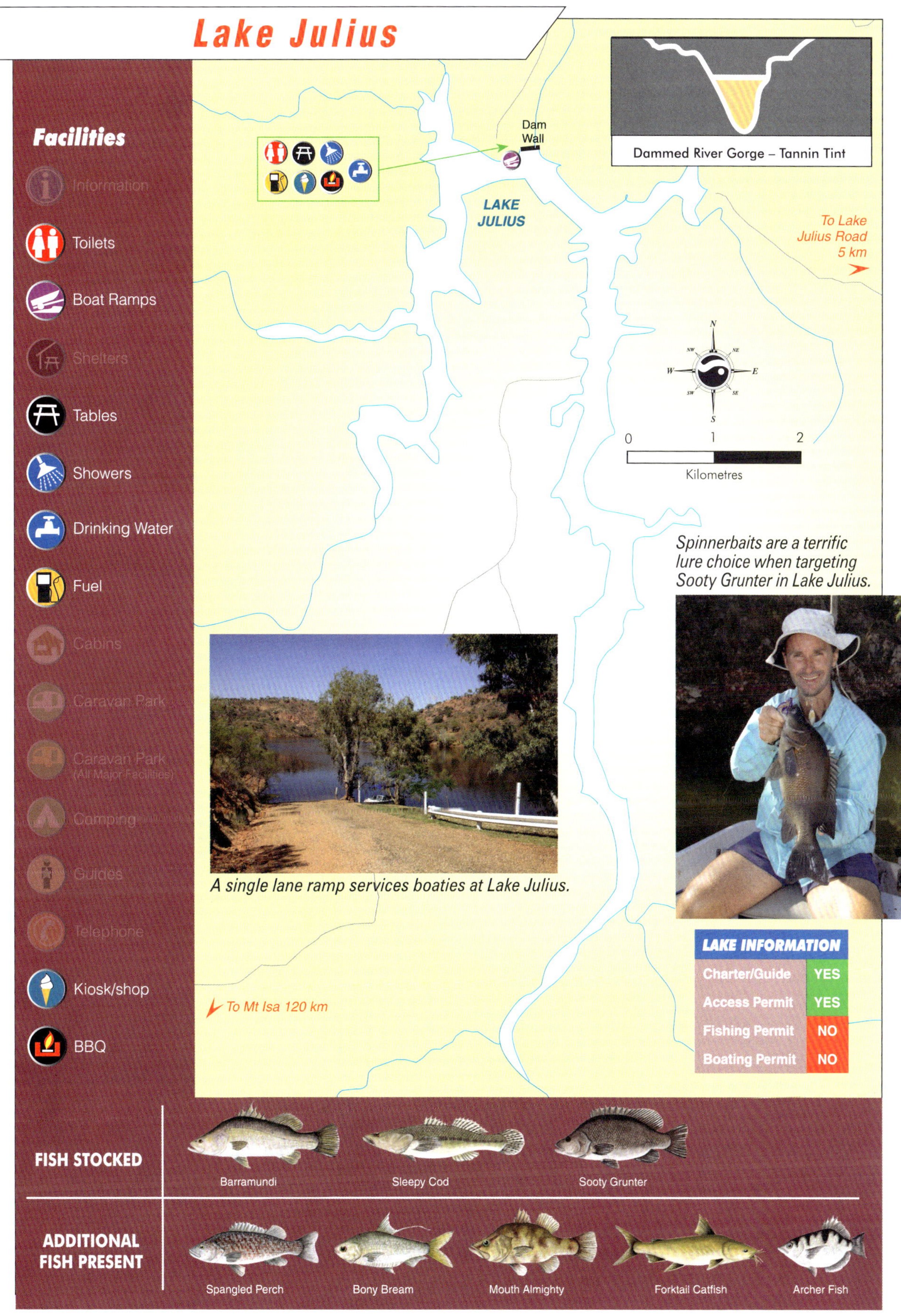

A single lane ramp services boaties at Lake Julius.

Spinnerbaits are a terrific lure choice when targeting Sooty Grunter in Lake Julius.

LAKE INFORMATION	
Charter/Guide	YES
Access Permit	YES
Fishing Permit	NO
Boating Permit	NO

Kidston Dam

About

Location The Lynd
Drainage Flinders River
Surface Area 500 ha
Capacity 20,000 ML
Usage Mining
Management (Not stocked as of 2008)
Contact for fishing permit: N/A

Weipa
Cooktown
CAIRNS
Kidston Dam
TOWNSVILLE
Mount Isa
Mackay
Rockhampton
Gladstone
Bundaberg
Fraser Island
Birdsville
Maroochydore
BRISBANE

This former water supply for mining operations around old Kidston town is built on Copperfield Creek in the Gilbert Range in the Northern Territory. Access is via a turn off at The Lynd, itself a major road junction in those parts. The lake lies an hour or so drive from the Oasis Roadhouse along a dirt road.

Kidston Dam

FISHING

Ardent anglers in love with the sooty grunter 'sock it to you' attitude to lures and flies will love the place where a naturally occurring population flourishes. Some sooties are of soccer ball proportions. Red claw crayfish and sleepy cod are also present. With the Gulf Country well on the way to an outback tourist boom, and the associated magnetism of well stocked lakes, finned enhancements at Copperfield are assured.

There are a few mining remnants around the lake but visitor facilities are scant. An amenities scarcity does not discourage Easter campers, rocking up with nets and freezers, from pegging out every available piece of flat ground. The remoteness of this lake and unlikelihood of apprehension makes Kidston a poacher's paradise. That will change with a visitor stream from further afield.

FACILITIES

There are toilets at the dam. The Oaks Rush Outback Resort is located 7 km from the old Kidston town and offers cabin accommodations with an outback flavour (07 4062 4100 or email oaksrush@bigpond.com). This accommodation was the original quarters for the workers of the Kidston Gold Mine, which is now closed. The rehabilitation of the mine has just been completed and the owners have transformed the workers accommodation into a unique outback resort.

BOATING

There is a boat ramp but the access road may require 4WD for access.

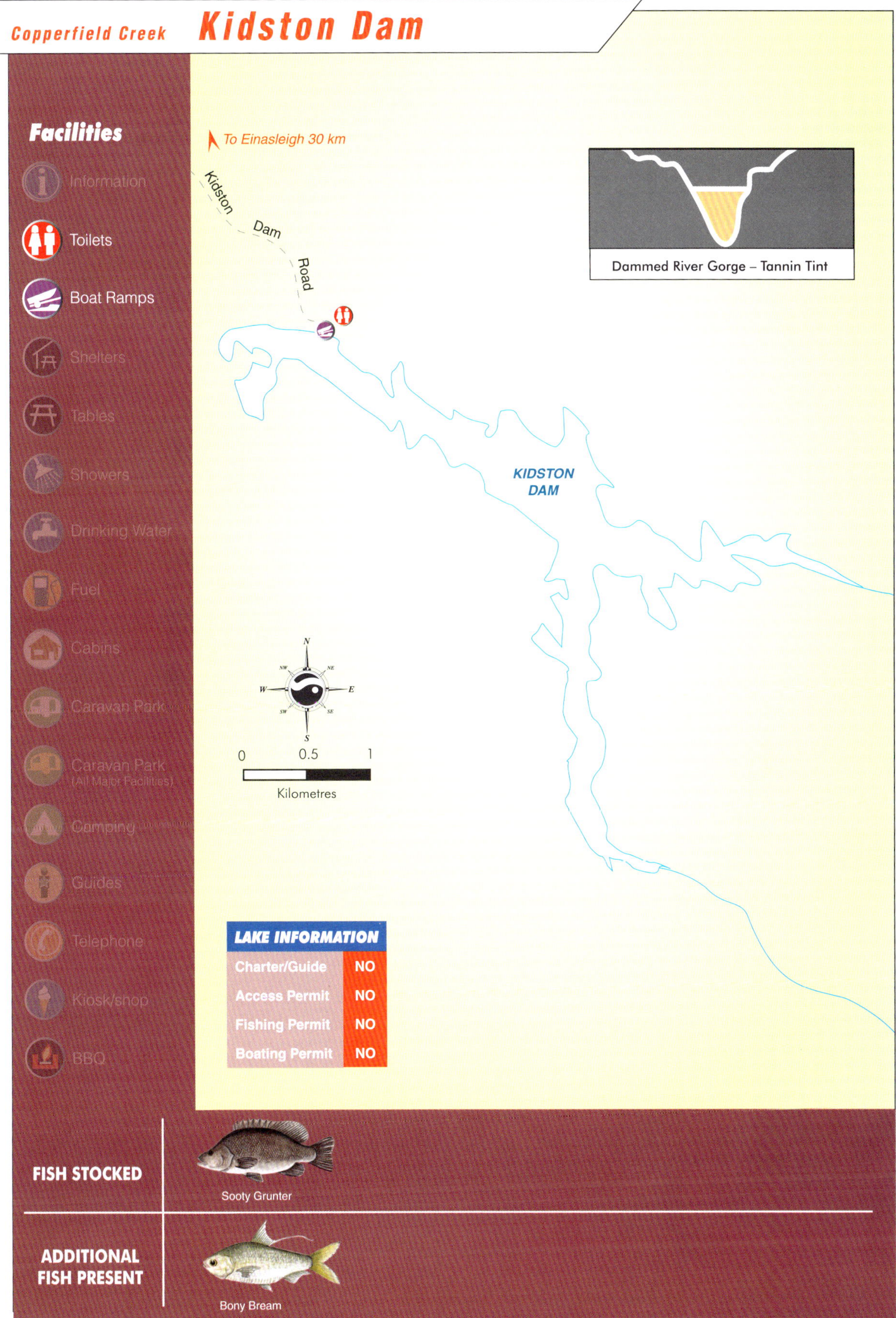
Copperfield Creek
Kidston Dam
Facilities
Information
Toilets
Boat Ramps
Shelters
Tables
Showers
Drinking Water
Fuel
Cabins
Caravan Park
Caravan Park (All Major Facilities)
Camping
Guides
Telephone
Kiosk/shop
BBQ
To Einasleigh 30 km
Kidston Dam Road
Dammed River Gorge – Tannin Tint
KIDSTON DAM
N
NE
E
SE
S
SW
W
NW
0
0.5
1
Kilometres
LAKE INFORMATION
Charter/Guide NO
Access Permit NO
Fishing Permit NO
Boating Permit NO
FISH STOCKED
Sooty Grunter
ADDITIONAL FISH PRESENT
Bony Bream

Kinchant Dam

Weipa
Cooktown
CAIRNS
TOWNSVILLE
Mount Isa
Kinchant Dam
Mackay
Rockhampton
Gladstone
Bundaberg
Fraser Island
Birdsville
Maroochydore
BRISBANE

About

Location	Mackay
Drainage	Pioneer System
Surface Area	920 ha
Capacity	62,800 ML
Usage	Irrigation & Town Water
Management	Sun Water 07 4783 0555

Contact for fishing permit: www.smartservice.qld.gov.au or Sun Water

This 'little brother' water to Teemburra is also located on the Pioneer River system 30 km west of Mackay. Kinchant Dam was built on Sandy Creek to provide irrigation and town water in 1977. To get to Kinchant Dam, travel west from Mackay through North Eton and follow the signs to the dam, which can also be accessed via a bitumen and dirt road from Mirani, past the Pioneer Valley Golf Course.

It is both well stocked (Mackay Area Fish Stocking Association) and well appointed. Relatively open water provides the less challenging fishing. This makes it an ideal place for the casual angler content to cast from the bank.

FISHING (Permit Required)

Fish stocked here are sooty grunter, sleepy cod and, since 2000, barramundi. There are also breeding populations of forktail catfish, eel-tailed catfish, spangled perch and mouth almighty.

Kinchant's status as a lesser lake can be a blessing in disguise. Anglers are more likely to have this water to themselves. Given the absolute need to a quiet approach when barra fishing in stillwaters, there may be less chance of some unwitting dolt ruining things.

Places like Kinchant highlight the value of small lures and lightweight presentations. These favour spin gear more than the baitcasters of barra tradition. Within the realm of mini lures, soft plastics with in-built weight provide realism and convenience. The upriding hook is less weed prone than a treble, but hits will be missed because of the rigid nature and placement. A presentation trick with soft plastics is to cast as flat as possible to minimise splashy impacts and rip the lure a foot or so the instant it lands. Barra don't like fake fish that sink on a bit of string before moving off. Neither should you, considering the reaction strikes that are missed.

The weedy nature of the lake makes surface luring over the tops of submerged weed a great option. Late afternoon sessions and into the night is the time to walk and bloop surface lures over this weed. Anglers who study the weed formations during the day are able to stealthily troll the weed edges at night with shallow running lures. This technique produces some of the lake's biggest barra on a regular basis. Fishing permits are available online.

Quality lure presentation can be the key to hooking big Kinchant Dam barra.

FACILITIES

There is a park area overlooking the dam, ideal for picnics with barbecues, toilets, a kiosk, licensed restaurant and cabins at the resort. Camping is permitted and fees apply. There is caravan park accommodation at the Kinchant Waters Leisure Resort 07 4954 1453

BOATING

There are no boating or speed limit restrictions here, thus it is very popular with the water ski fraternity. A concrete boat ramp is provided.

Kinchant Dam

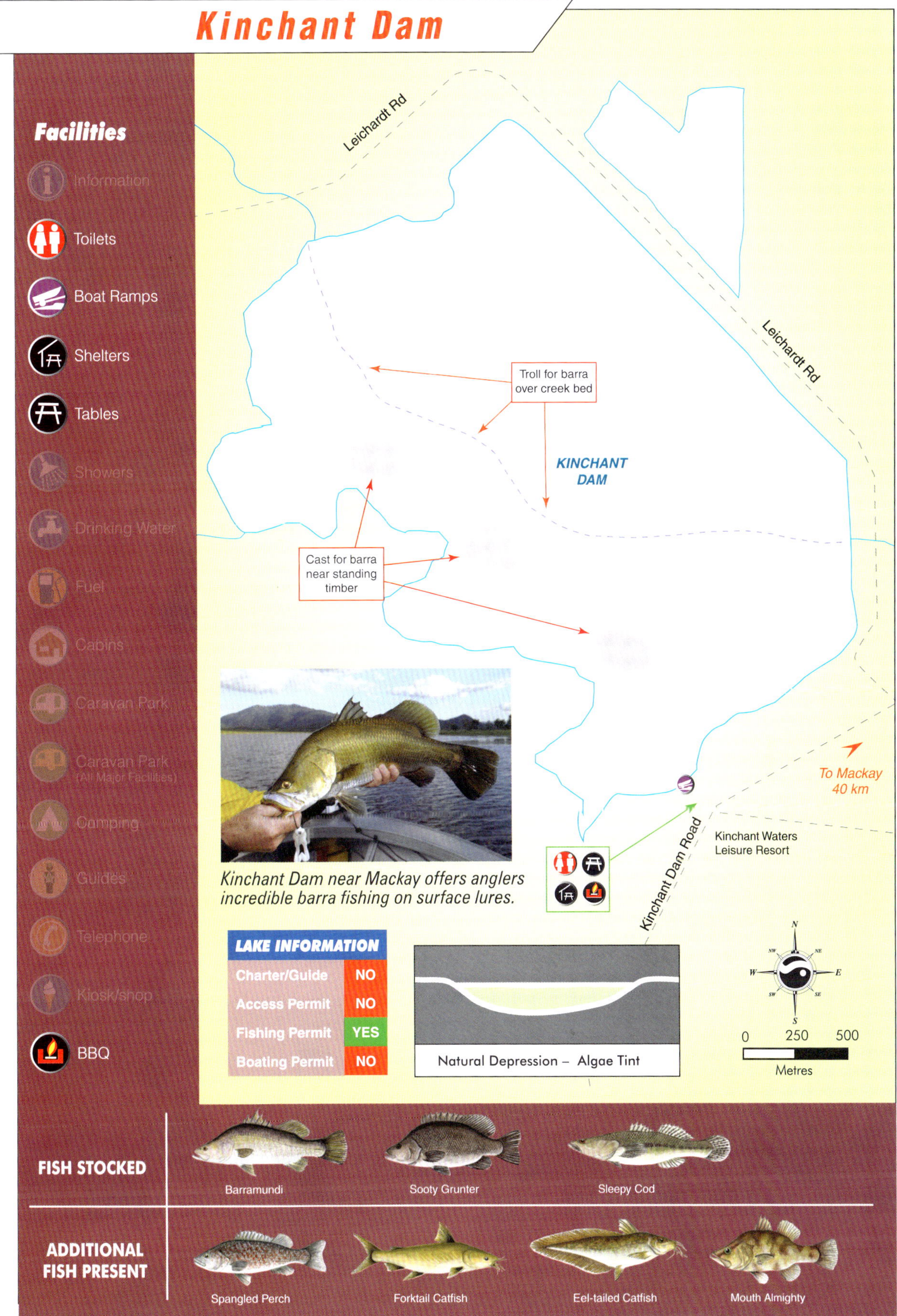

Kinchant Dam near Mackay offers anglers incredible barra fishing on surface lures.

LAKE INFORMATION	
Charter/Guide	NO
Access Permit	NO
Fishing Permit	YES
Boating Permit	NO

Lake Koombooloomba

About

Location	Ravenshoe
Drainage	Tully River
Surface Area	1560 ha
Capacity	200,500 ML
Usage	Hydro
Management	Stanwell Corporation Ltd 07 4051 4258

Contact for fishing permit: N/A

Nestled in rainforest near Ravenshoe, this lake that's so often shrouded in mist has a distinctive jade colour. It has been stocked with both barramundi and sooty grunter. Indications are that conditions in this somewhat isolated lake are better suited to the latter.

FISHING

The damp terrain makes access difficult, if not impossible, and boat launching quite out of the question. Though lightly fished, Koombooloomba isn't an easy lake. Barramundi have to be regarded more as a (welcome) by-catch rather than a primary target. Switched on anglers have a knack for targeting the lake's barra which love any hard structure. Smaller offerings seem to be their undoing especially when water temperatures are cooler.

In times of rain excellent sooty fishing can be found in the dams headwaters. Casting spinnerbaits, blades and small diving minnows into the running water can produce some frantic action. And the charcoal black sooty grunter deserves to be regarded as smart fish that make themselves scarce where fishermen become obvious. A boat is a prerequisite.

Besides stealth, the capacity to make long searching casts is essential. Casts that are made ahead of the boat stand a much better change than those behind. As the boat arrives into the near periphery of a specific location, the element of surprise tends to be surrendered. The really endearing thing about sooty grunter—besides their jolting strike—is their very loose preferences in lures. If ever a fish bridged the gap between inland and tropical sportfish it's these hardy finned black tanks. Barra minnows, broad bib wobblers, spinnerbaits, soft plastics, a hunk of meat—it doesn't matter. The important thing, to harp, is that presentations be the first thing to get the their attention.

FACILITIES

There is a camping area at the lake with limited facilities, pit toilets only.

BOATING

There are no boating restrictions and there is an unsealed ramp.

Picturesque Koombooloomba Lake holds plentiful numbers of Sooty Grunter and the odd barramundi.

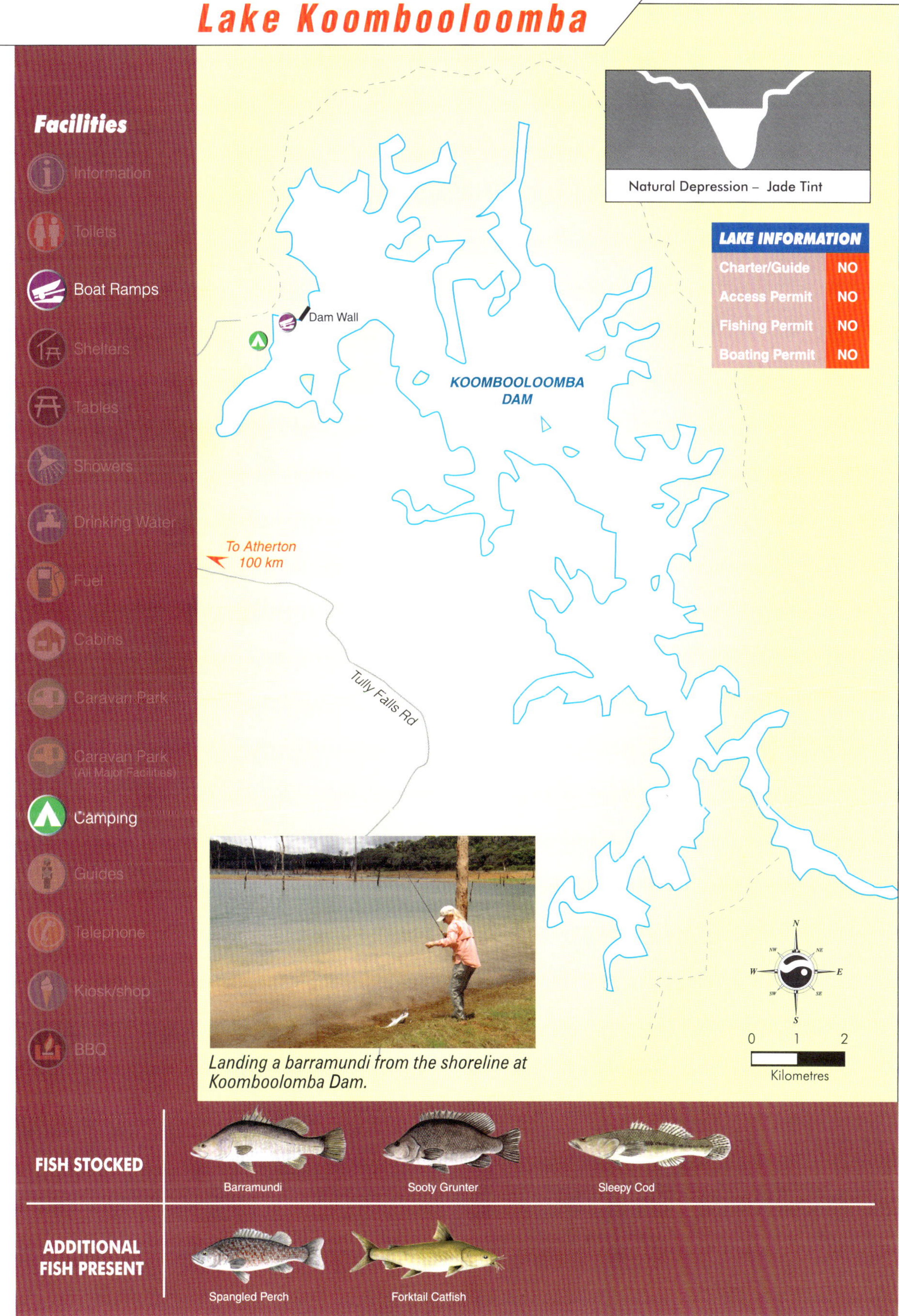

Landing a barramundi from the shoreline at Koomboolomba Dam.

Lake Kurwongbah

Weipa
Cooktown
CAIRNS
TOWNSVILLE
Mount Isa
Mackay
Rockhampton
Gladstone
Bundaberg
Fraser Island
Birdsville
Maroochydore
Lake Kurwongbah
BRISBANE

About

Location	Brisbane
Drainage	North Pine River
Surface Area	320 ha
Capacity	14,500 ML
Usage	Domestic
Management	Moreton Bay Regional Council

Contact for fishing permit: N/A

Lake Kurwongbah is peaceful stillwater sited in peaceful parklands in the leafy suburb bearing the same name is a great place to take kids fishing. Built in 1984 on Sideling Creek, a tributary of the North Pine River, Kurwongbah has been heavily stocked with bass, golden perch and saratoga. The stocking program is well funded and the initial stockings produced quality fish with fast growth rates. These fish will take some years to reach trophy size but numbers will make up for this. The near proximity of this water to northern Brisbane suburbia will ensure it's future as a fishing hole once stockings mature.

Tilapia found in Kurwongbah are declared noxious fish and should not be returned to the water.

FISHING

The stocking of saratoga, bass and golden perch has given anglers the opportunity to tangle with something special. The lake was already loaded with the noxious species, tilapia, before stocking commenced. The stocked fish seem to favour the edges of the lake which makes them accessible to anglers fishing from the shore. Structure in the shallows seems to hold plenty of fish and tossing lures around the weed, lilies and other cover is a great way to entice them. Blades, plastics, spinnerbaits and small hardbodies are ideal throughout the morning and afternoon. During periods of low light, bass and saratoga are willing to pounce on surface lures. The initial stockings of saratoga saw fingerlings and fully mature breeding fish released. After some good seasons, these fish should now have established a stronger breeding population.

It should be noted that cabomba weed, which is a threatening non-native plant, has been detected in the dam. Items such as traps should be washed and aired in the sun for several days to prevent the spread of this pest.

FACILITIES

The eastern shoreline is easily accessed along Dayboro Road. Well appointed picnic facilities have been installed at Mick Hanfling Park. These include picnic shelters and tables, electric barbecues and toilets. Ample vehicle parking spaces are provided and the open grassed areas that extend to the water are for play or a cast.

BOATING

Bank launched paddle and electric motor powered boats are permitted. The local water ski club operates high horsepower powered craft and at this writing negotiations are in progress with the controlling authority for equivalent angler access.

The stocking of natives will hopefully help control the outbreak of noxious fish.

Lake Kurwongbah

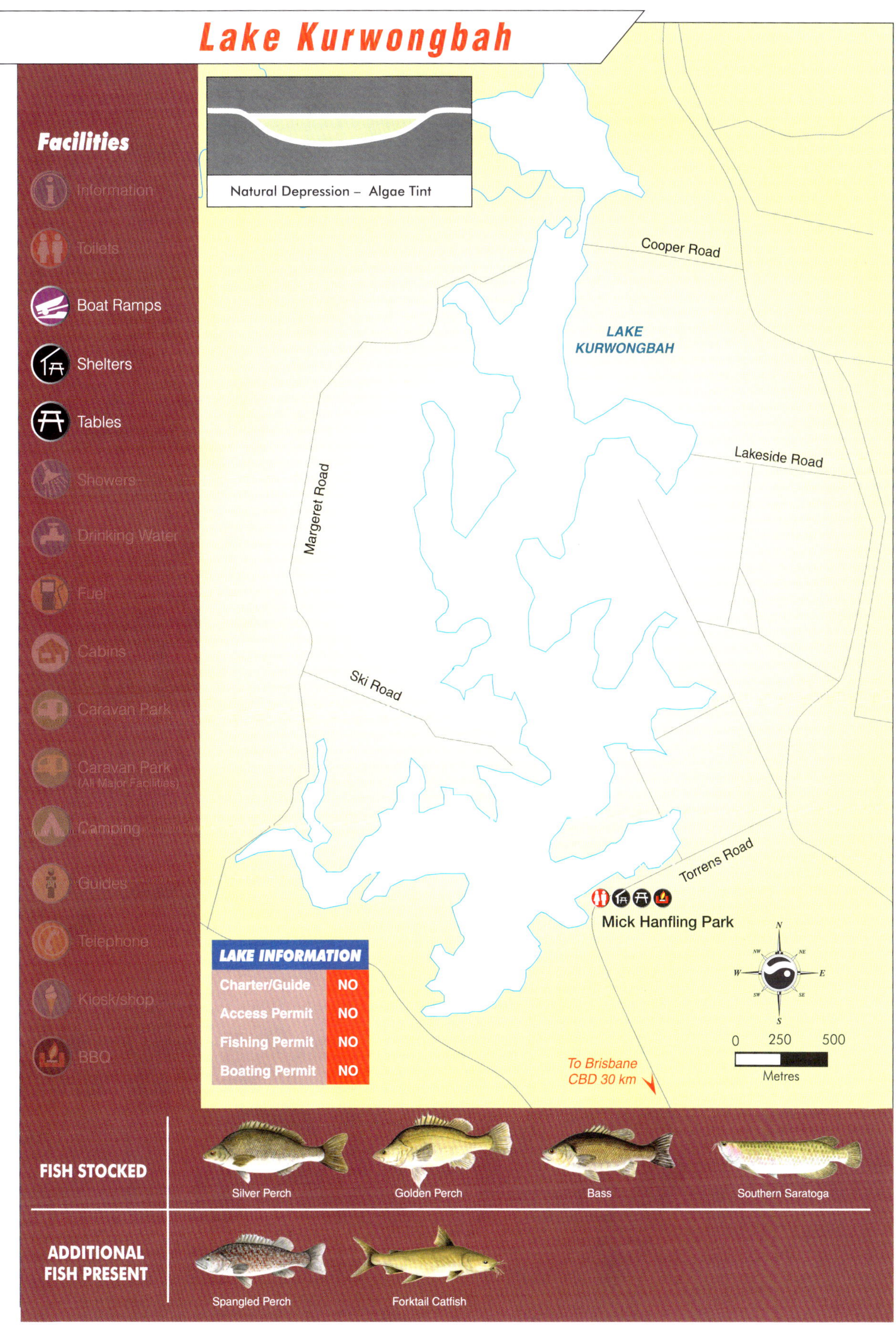

LAKE INFORMATION	
Charter/Guide	NO
Access Permit	NO
Fishing Permit	NO
Boating Permit	NO

Lake Lenthall

About

Location	Mackay
Drainage	Pioneer System
Surface Area	920 ha
Capacity	62,800 ML
Usage	Irrigation & Town Water
Management	Sun Water 07 4783 0555

Contact for fishing permit: www.smartservice.qld.gov.au or Sun Water

Weipa
Cooktown
CAIRNS
TOWNSVILLE
Mount Isa
Mackay
Rockhampton
Gladstone
Bundaberg
Lake Lenthall
Fraser Island
Birdsville
Maroochydore
BRISBANE

Named after one the region's pioneering families, picturesque Lenthall is the southernmost lake to be officially stocked with barramundi. The road into the lake from the Bruce Highway can be potholed and juddering, however facilities at the water have recently been expanded. Amongst the prettiest lakes, Lenthall is surrounded by casuarinas and paper barks, their soft colours making an eye-catching contrast against the margin of green water lily pads and tannin stained water. Atmosphere? You bet!

FISHING

(Permit Required)

Be that as it may, the Lenthall Fish Stocking Association sees their water as primarily a bass fishery with stocking mixes heavily weighted in that direction. Saratoga have been added to the Lenthall cocktail. If and when they establish into a self sustaining stock, and the ignorant notion is seen off that barra shouldn't be stocked 'because they eat bass' fishing quality at Lenthall will indeed match the scenery. Of course, barra will eat any fish that'll fit inside their cavernous mouths—but little bass are much more adept at avoiding predation than the abundant forage fish in Queensland lakes. Other fish stocked and present include golden perch and silver perch.

Over the years, floods have caused the dam to run over the spillway and give many mature fish a free ride to the weirs and river system below. Constant stocking sees new fish introduced so there is always something to catch and some of the lake's older and bigger fish are always a chance.

FACILITIES

There is an onsite ranger at the dam, plus toilets, picnic tables, camping sites, fishing platform and boat ramp. Motel and caravan park accommodation is available in Maryborough. Access to the dam can be rough and corrugated so take your time and look out for wildlife.

BOATING

Speed and engine restrictions are in place and boats can only use the dam from 6 a.m. to 8 p.m. Low emission engines with a 2 or 3 star rating which are below 60 hp are allowed on the lake. All 4 strokes and low emission direct injection 2 strokes fall into this category. Paddle craft and electric powered boats can be used as well.

Kayaking is a terrific way of experiencing Lenthalls Dam and offers a stealthy, quiet approach which is less likely to spook fish.

Lake Lenthall

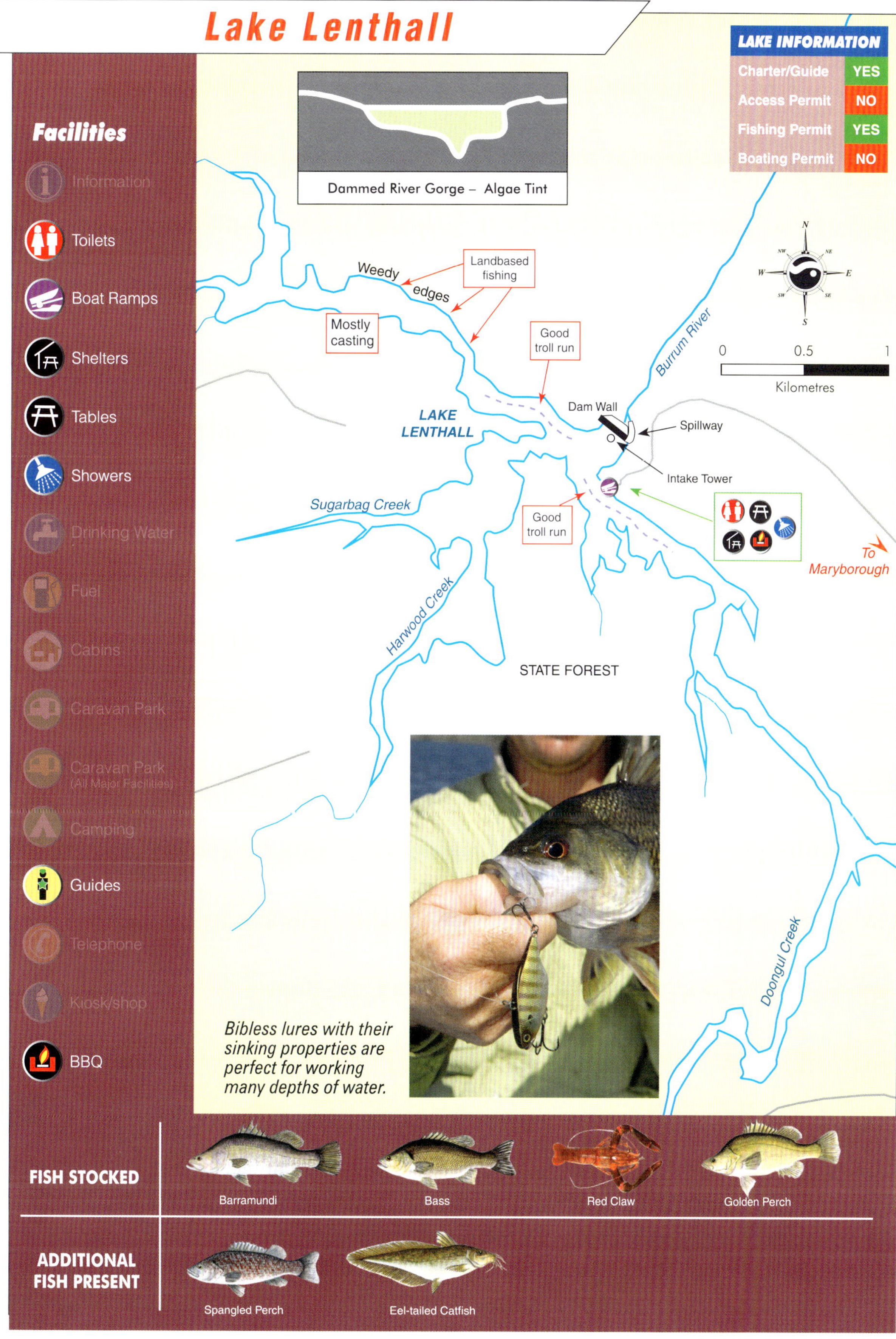

Bibless lures with their sinking properties are perfect for working many depths of water.

Leslie Dam

About

Location	Warwick
Drainage	Murray Darling
Surface Area	1,260 ha
Capacity	106,000 ML
Usage	Irrigation
Management	Sun Water 07 3884 5317

Contact for fishing permit: www.smartservice.qld.gov.au or Sun Water

Situated approximately 15 km west of Warwick, Leslie Dam has been one of Queensland's most popular freshwater destinations for many years. Named after the pioneer Leslie family, this bland looking lake was built in 1963 across Sandy Creek, a tributary of the Condamine River. Since the 1990s the lake has been heavily stocked with natives. Lake Leslie has an average depth of 8.4 metres.

FISHING (Permit Required)

A no fishing zone is in place at the dam wall.

The local fish stocking group have worked tirelessly to stock large numbers of golden perch, silver perch and Murray cod to bolster the natural populations of spangled perch and eel-tailed catfish. Golden perch dominate most catches for lure / fly anglers, while silver perch and eel-tailed catfish are more of a baitfishing prospect.

There are many large boulders around the fringes and some standing timber in the upper reaches of Sandy Creek so care should be taken when navigating in these areas. Breeding 'structure' in the form of tractor tyres has been added to the lake to assist Murray cod breeding. The odd boulder outcrop punctuates the lake fringes and there is standing timber in the upper reaches of Sandy Creek. Yellowbelly dominate captures with lures and bait both effective.

When full, and firing, catch statistics from Leslie have been the highest, per angler hour, of any stocked lake. An astounding statistic was that 70 per cent of the golden perch liberated were being caught! With the general lack of cover in the main basin, covering water becomes the name of the game. The most effort effective way is to troll. Any number of small to medium sized, big bib diving lures will handle the task.

The location of boulders is worth noting...along with the closer attention that goes with casts. The majority of cod taken in Leslie come from those locations. Cod being cod, as one is caught, another moves in. The standing timber along upper Sandy Creek attracts schools of yellowbelly when the water level creates depths between three and five metres. Bait fishers tie up and bag out. Live and fresh shrimp is by far the best bait. Presentations are enhanced through a slight up and down bobbing motion, that action being provided through the rod tip.

FACILITIES

There is bush camping permitted beside the water at Washpools and Sandy Creek reserves where basic facilities are provided—fees apply, 07 4661 3406.

Other facilities at the dam wall include toilets, barbecues, drinking water, bait and ice. SunWater staff are on site.

BOATING

There are no boating restrictions on Lake Leslie. There is a concrete boat launching ramp provided not far from the dam wall. When water levels are low boats can still be launched from this area with some care. A four wheel drive may be required. Alternatively, boats may be launched from the Washpools reserve, however a four wheel drive is recommended here.

Leslie Dam at capacity.

Leslie Dam

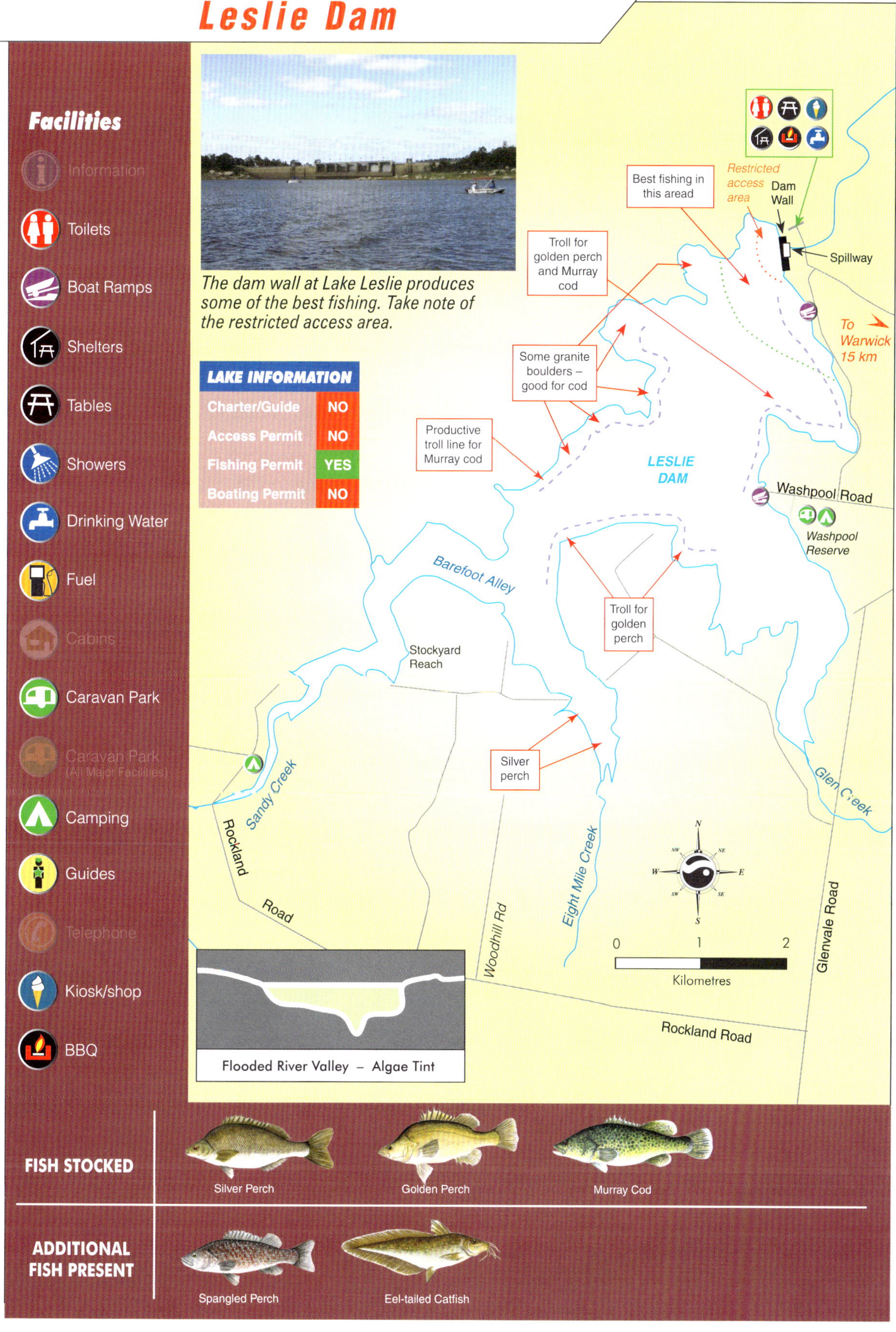

The dam wall at Lake Leslie produces some of the best fishing. Take note of the restricted access area.

LAKE INFORMATION	
Charter/Guide	NO
Access Permit	NO
Fishing Permit	YES
Boating Permit	NO

Lake MacDonald

Weipa
Cooktown
CAIRNS
TOWNSVILLE
Mount Isa
Mackay
Rockhampton
Gladstone
Bundaberg
Fraser Island
Birdsville
Lake MacDonald
Maroochydore
BRISBANE

About

Location	Cooroy
Drainage	Six Mile Creek
Surface Area	260 ha
Capacity	15,500 ML
Usage	Domestic / Agriculture
Management	Sunshine Coast Regional Council 07 5449 5200

Contact for fishing permit: Sunshine Coast Regional Council

Sited on Six Mile Creek, a Mary River tributary in the Sunshine Coast hinterland, Lake McDonald is a relatively shallow but extremely weedy lake. Heavy shoreline growths make bankside fishing difficult, if not impossible. This abundant aquatic plant life forms the basis of a very rich food chain, which in turn produces beautifully conditioned fish. Luckless anglers could well be talking about MacDonald whenever citing the one about fish having too much to eat.

FISHING (Permit Required)

The adjacent Gerry Cook Fish Hatchery is operated by the local fish stocking group in conjunction with the Noosa Shire Council. It carries on important preservation and re-stocking work on the endangered Mary River cod. A breeding population has been established but possession/ taking is totally prohibited. Lake MacDonald also holds bass, golden perch and silver perch. Weedy conditions favour casting rather than trolling. Best results come from casting lures from small boats back towards shoreline weedbeds. The fishing challenge can be twofold. Good weed avoidance tactics are called for as skilled anglers able to make weedless presentations with lure, fly or bait then have to extract fish that bury themselves in dense weed clusters.

In the cooler months bass can be found schooling in the deeper water. A sounder will reveal the location of these fish which are usually quite willing to eat a soft plastic or blade bait. The area near the dam wall and around the water bubbler is always worth exploring. Fish will often migrate to the lower end of the lake following heavy rain and a rise in water level.

Saratoga are always a good possibility. These fish love to hunt the lake's structure. Casting spinnerbaits and lightly weighted plastics in Borer Creek is often successful.

The local fish stocking group is the Lake MacDonald Fish Management Committee, Box 108, Pomona, Qld, 4468.

FACILITIES

There are some picnic facilities at the lake. Camping is not permitted.

BOATING

Paddle powered craft and electric motors are allowed. However, outbreaks of noxious weed, which can be transferred to other waters via boats and trailers is both cause for alarm and an access review. Information Noosa Shire Council 07 5449 5200.

Yellowbelly frequently feed around weedbeds in Lake MacDonald.

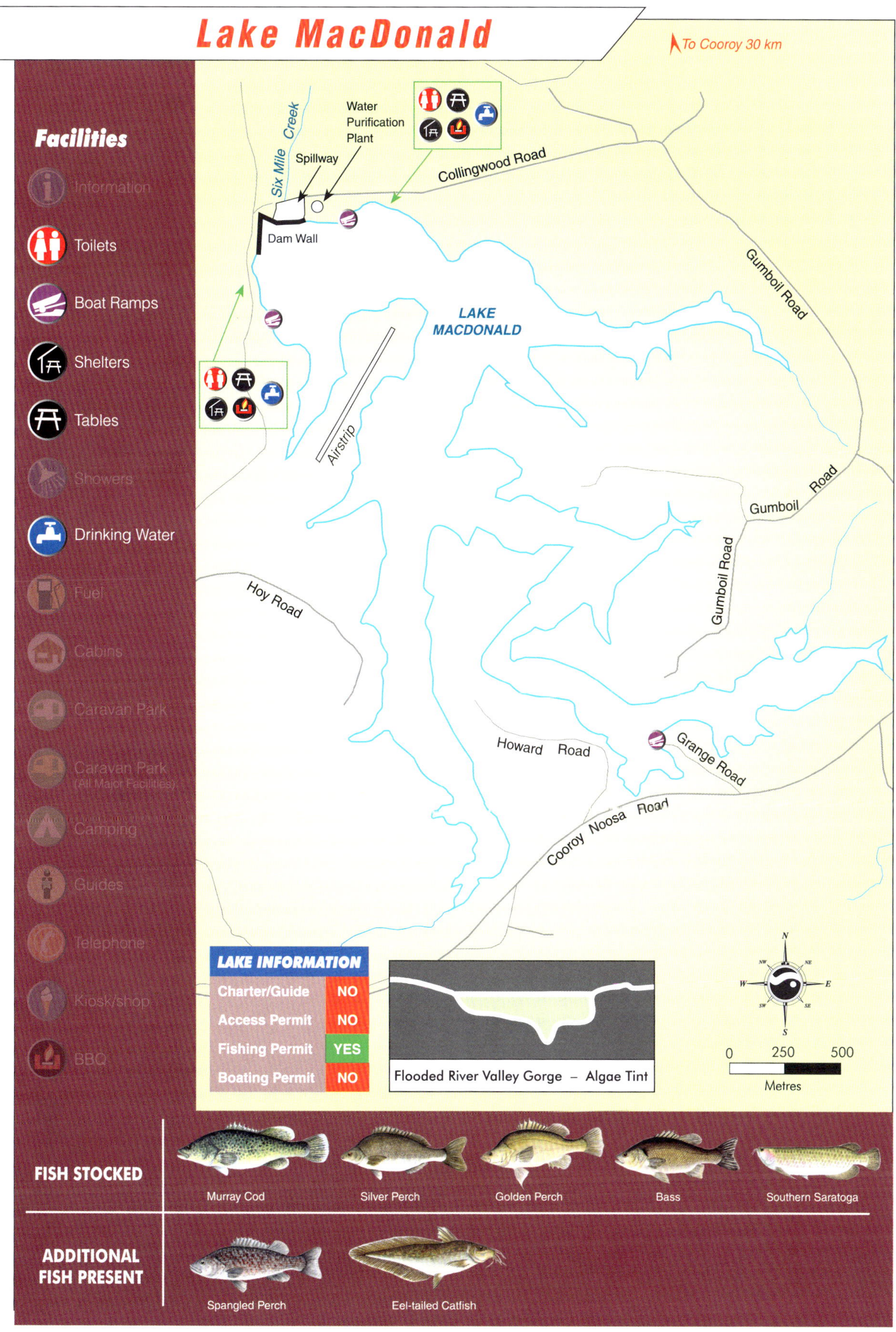
Lake MacDonald
To Cooroy 30 km
Facilities
Information
Toilets
Boat Ramps
Shelters
Tables
Showers
Drinking Water
Fuel
Cabins
Caravan Park
Caravan Park
(All Major Facilities)
Camping
Guides
Telephone
Kiosk/shop
BBQ
Water
Purification
Plant
Six Mile Creek
Spillway
Dam Wall
Collingwood Road
Gumboil Road
LAKE
MACDONALD
Airstrip
Gumboil Road
Gumboil Road
Hoy Road
Howard Road
Grange Road
Cooroy Noosa Road
LAKE INFORMATION
Charter/Guide NO
Access Permit NO
Fishing Permit YES
Boating Permit NO
Flooded River Valley Gorge – Algae Tint
N
NW
NE
W
E
SW
SE
S
0 250 500
Metres
FISH STOCKED
Murray Cod
Silver Perch
Golden Perch
Bass
Southern Saratoga
ADDITIONAL FISH PRESENT
Spangled Perch
Eel-tailed Catfish

Lake Maroon

Weipa
Cooktown
CAIRNS
TOWNSVILLE
Mount Isa
Mackay
Rockhampton
Gladstone
Bundaberg
Fraser Island
Birdsville
Maroochydore
BRISBANE
Lake Maroon

About

Location	Boonah
Drainage	Logan River
Surface Area	350 ha
Capacity	22,500 ML
Usage	Domestic / Agriculture
Management	Sun Water 07 3884 5317

Contact for fishing permit: www.smartservice.qld.gov.au or Sun Water

Sited amid pleasant surrounds of Burnett Creek, a Logan River feeder, Maroon is a well stocked lake that's kind to anglers. This relatively shallow lake has extensive weed margins that make boats a necessity. Maroon is lightly fished compared with its bigger, sister lake, Moogerah. This situation is because of the bass not being as big. There are no bony bream—protein filled growth pills, you can be sure—in Maroon. The compact nature of this lake places some limits on the number of boats. While not in a regulatory sense, the presence of a half dozen craft would have to lower confidence levels as optimism is hard to find on second hand water.

FISHING (Permit Required)

Fundamentally, a bass fishery where 40 cm plus fish can be regarded as big, Maroon has also been stocked with the major natives. There isn't a great deal of hard cover, most angler effort is concentrated on the edges of shoreline weedbeds where the greater casting distances possible sees spinnerbaits on more rods than hardbody minnows and wobblers.

The rear of the lake has a couple of hectares where there are inviting bankside vegetation overhangs. This location is a consistent producer and is popular with flyfishers making surface presentations. The periods of half light around dawn and dusk are the best fishing times. It should be noted the official hours for boating are 6 a.m. until 6 p.m. The fish out feeding can be encountered around the shallower lake fringes but as the light intensifies, they tend to retreat to deeper water.

The local fish stocking group is Maroon Moogerah Fish Management Assn, 1 Railway St Kalbar Qld, 4309.

FACILITIES

There are no visitor facilities at this lake, nor provision for camping. Accomodation and tent sites are at Pointro Camp Ground which is accessed via Burnett Creek Road on the south eastern side of the lake. Phone 07 5463 6209.

BOATING

Maroon has a concrete boat ramp and is not subject to any boating restrictions. At low levels the concrete ramp is well above water level and boats need to be launched from the bank. 4WD vehicles are best for this although cars should be fine with smaller boats. Rain can make the banks slippery for retrieving boats. The boat ramp found at Pointro Campground is solid dirt and gravel.

Early morning mist on Lake Maroon.

Lake Maroon

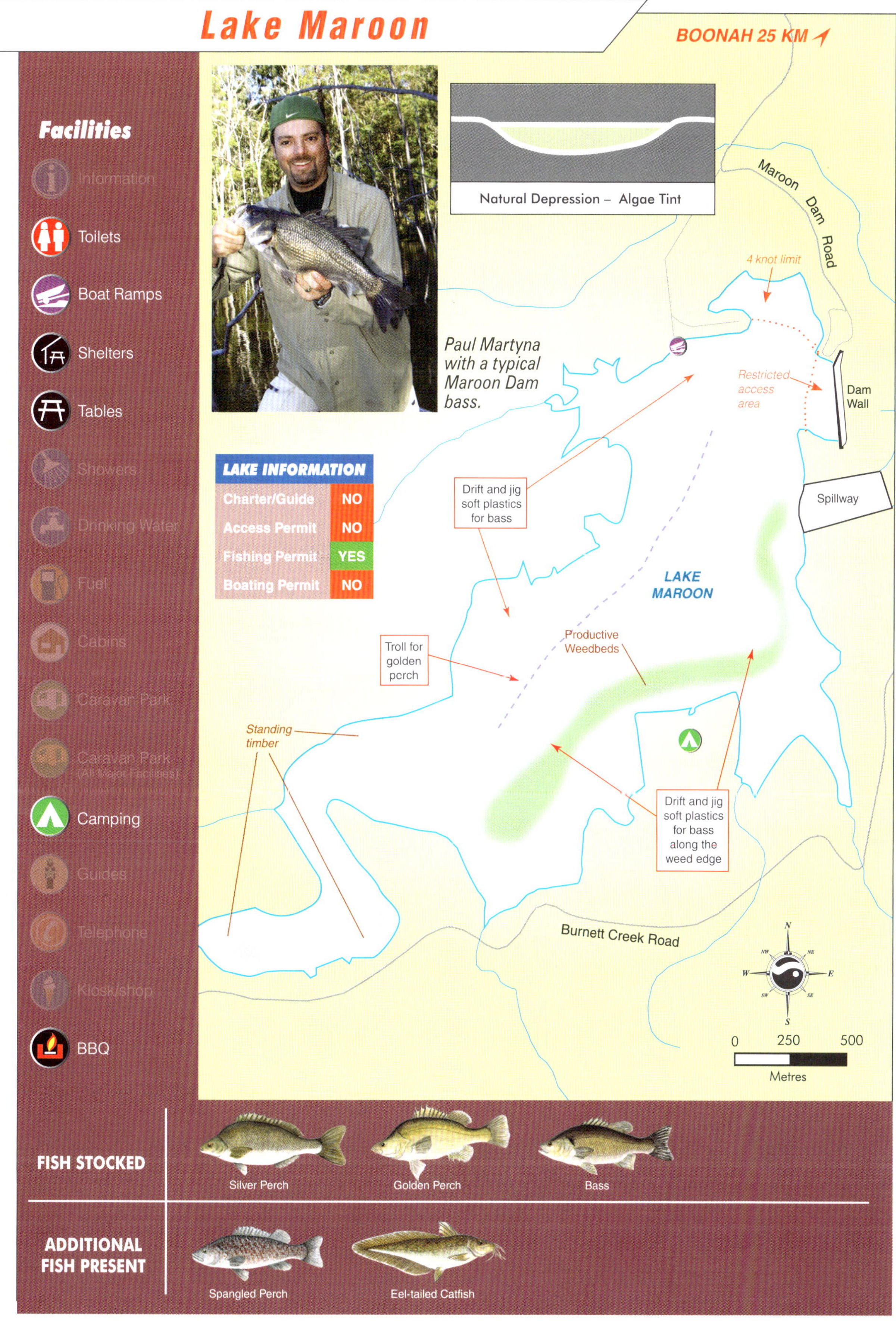

Paul Martyna with a typical Maroon Dam bass.

Lake Monduran

About

Location	Gin Gin
Drainage	Burnett River
Surface Area	5350 ha
Capacity	585,000 ML
Usage	Irrigation / Domestic
Management	Sun Water 07 4132 6200

Contact for fishing permit: www.smartservice.qld.gov.au or Sun Water

Monduran is a narrow-gutted dam with heavily timbered fringes. Combined with numbers of dead-end back alley bays, the disorienting effect has been sufficient for people to become lost. Once plagued by forktail catfish, Monduran has matured to overtake (for the time being, anyway) Awoonga in terms of boat trailers at the ramp. An initial stocking of sooty grunter, golden perch and silver perch didn't work. Bass did—evidenced enough by the 50+ cm fish being caught.

FISHING (Permit Required)

However, it's the barra that people come for and through '06 to '10 Monduran didn't disappoint. The November full moon has been the time to hit the lake early in the morning and again late into the night. This moon draws lots of monster barra to the main basin of the lake away from the snags. Here, they can be easily trolled up on hardbodied diving lures. As happens with all booming lake fisheries there's a plateau in fishing quality, and more difficult days ahead as fish become educated.

Casting anglers are challenged by the sticks. There's more to it than accuracy and handling bitchy braids in the wind. Tempting as the bigger trees are, my advice is to concentrate on the 'sticky' ones instead—lantana tangles are a special! Small branches develop algal growths quicker. Those coatings attract browsing bony bream and enhance the cover potential...cover and food, all wrapped in one...say no more!

Barra roam freely through the sticks and chances of hooking one can be increased by positioning the boat on a prominent point or submerged hump. In these areas, look for openings in the trees to cast to. Hooking a fish in the open will give you a fighting chance of landing it without having to unwind it from all the trees. Side imaging sounder technology has given barra anglers more confidence when working these points and waiting for cruising fish.

FACILITIES

Facilities include toilets, wood and electric barbecues and picnic tables and drinking water. The Lake Monduran Holiday Park, 07 4157 3881, provides excellent powered and unpowered camp sites overlooking the lake. There are cabins, holiday houses, hire boats, tackle shop, general store and a full range of facilities.

BOATING

Open to all boats and no restrictions apply. There is a single ramp boat ramp.

The lure of snaring huge barra amongst the drowned timber at Monduran draws anglers from far and wide.

Fred Haigh Dam

Lake Monduran

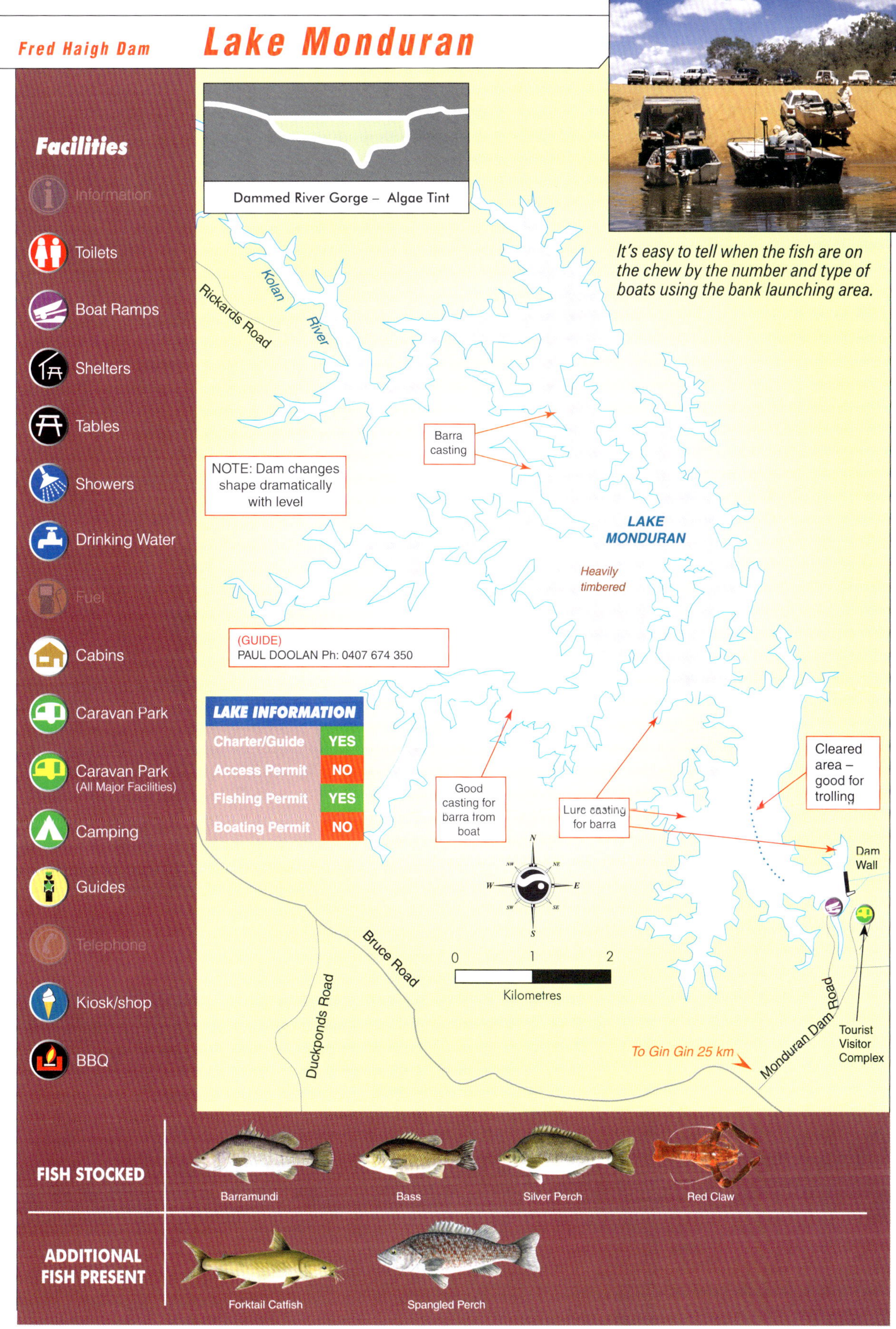

It's easy to tell when the fish are on the chew by the number and type of boats using the bank launching area.

LAKE INFORMATION	
Charter/Guide	YES
Access Permit	NO
Fishing Permit	YES
Boating Permit	NO

Lake Moogerah

Weipa
Cooktown
CAIRNS
TOWNSVILLE
Mount Isa
Mackay
Rockhampton
Gladstone
Bundaberg
Fraser Island
Birdsville
Maroochydore
BRISBANE
Lake Moogerah

About

Location	Ipswitch
Drainage	Brisbane River
Surface Area	880 ha
Capacity	92,500 ML
Usage	Water Supply & Irrigation
Management	Sun Water 07 3884 5317

Contact for fishing permit: www.smartservice.qld.gov.au or Sun Water

The name Moogerah is an aboriginal word meaning 'place of thunder storms'. How true, some of the blackest, brightest and most frightening storm cells imaginable rip across that part of the Gold Coast hinterland. Sited on the upper Bremer River and one of south east Queensland's more established stillwater fisheries, Moogerah hosts a variety of fish habitat. The Gorge is an appropriately named location from which rock fill for the dam wall was quarried. It is characterised by steep rock faces. Strikers Point is another fitting name and the Junction refers to the former confluence of Coulson and Reynolds creeks. An area of standing timber towards the rear of the lake is productive, especially when being used as staircases by hatching mudeyes on the march.

FISHING (Permit Required)

The presence of bony bream biomass assures rapid growth rates. Moogerah is a producer of 50 cm class bass, and along with goldens and silvers holds a breeding population of Mary River cod. Small numbers of saratoga have yet to indicate a successful stocking.

The dam has suffered from low levels in the past and sudden rises have contributed to fish kills. Some of the older, better quality fish are still there to be caught along with plenty of the fast growing smaller ones. When water levels are high, the start of the timber is a good place to cast and troll lipless crankbaits, blades and medium to deep diving lures. The spit near the boat ramp is worth a look but be prepared to dodge ski boats and get rocked around. When the water level drops, look along the flats which drop off into the old creek bed. Casters and trollers are divided along lines of skill and experience. Trolled small diving lures will take fish but not in the numbers of experienced anglers working with a full lure arsenal. The local fish stocking group is the Maroon Moogerah Fish Management Assn, PO Box 33 Kalbar, Qld, 4309.

FACILITIES

Facilities include toilets, kiosk, public telephone, wood and electric barbecues, picnic tables, drinking water. The nearby A G Muller Caravan Park 07 5463 0141 is fully appointed.

BOATING

The gates at A G Muller Park which provide access to the boat ramp open at 6 a.m. and close at 6 p.m.

There are no boating restrictions on Moogerah and this in turn attracts numbers of water skiers, especially during weekends and holidays. The boat wake and prop wash from those activities isn't conducive to peaceful fishing, nor is the excess decibels from high revving engines.

A beautifully coloured Mary River cod is carefully released.

Lake Moogerah

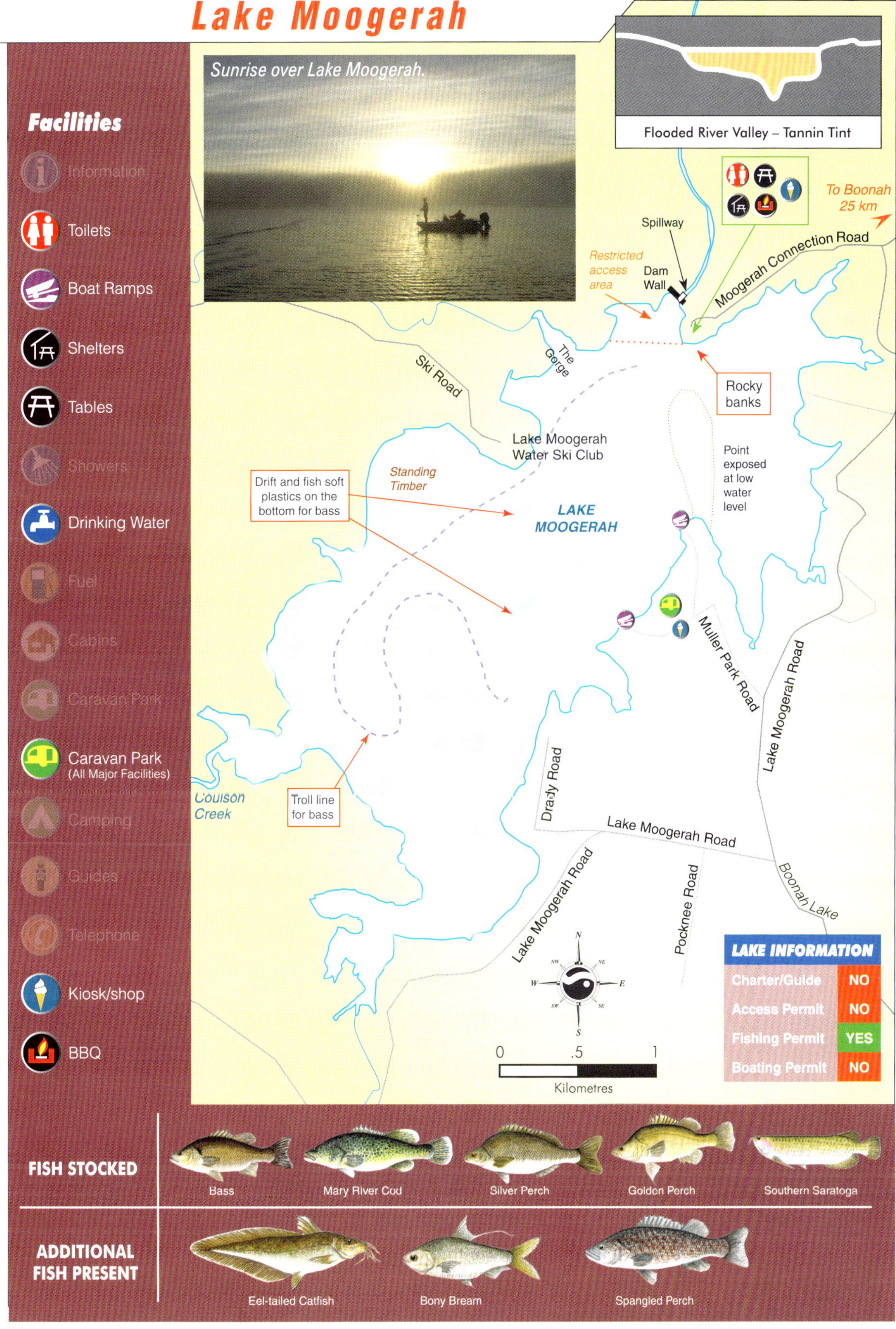

Lake Moondarra

About

Location	Mt Isa
Drainage	Leichhardt River
Surface Area	2375 ha
Capacity	107,000 ML
Usage	Town Water & Industrial
Management	Mount Isa City Council 07 4747 3200

Contact for fishing permit: N/A

Mt Isa Mines built Lake Moondarra in 1957 on the West Leichhardt River. The lake's name came from a public contest held at the time. Moondarra is an outback showpiece that's located 15 km north east of Mt Isa by sealed road. Moondarra serves Mt Isa's domestic and industrial needs as well as the recreational.

The lake is used for various recreational activities such as canoeing, sailing, boating, skiing, swimming, picnics and, increasingly, fishing. The lake is also the main source of fresh water for Mount Isa and a Fresh Water Lagoon was built to allow the water to naturally filter through reeds and for particles to settle out before pumping to Mount Isa.

The Mount Isa Fish Stocking and Management Group (MIFSG) operate a hatchery at Fresh Water Lagoon. Unfortunately, the absence of brackish water restricts fingerling production to sooty grunter. Barra fry are air lifted from coastal breeders.

The stocking group works tirelessly to ensure there are always fish in the dam. When the dam spilled over in 2009, surviving fish were netted under permit and placed back into the dam.

Moondarra at sunset.

FISHING

Fish from the 2004 year class now exceed the metre magic mark. Moondarra is subject to winter temperature extremes that will bring on fish kills and didn't escape the winter of '07. Barra escapes happened when flooding overran the lake, however Lake Julius, also in the Leichhardt River but further downstream, was a probable beneficiary of that exodus. Losses through high water and low temperatures are part of the package when it comes to barra stocking. They are, fortunately, not annual events and fade as progressive stocking groups get on with things. Trolling is popular amongst newcomer and casual anglers. The Isa has many gulf veterans who've cut their teeth in Carpentaria's tidal rivers. They've quickly picked up on the extensive nocturnal movements of lake fish during the warmer months and exploit the situation in shoreline casting sessions. Location is the key, and Moondarra has its share of little rocky spurs where fish pass within casting distance.

FACILITIES

There are toilets, picnic tables, barbecues, drinking water and shelters. There is no camping at the dam but 13 km away located on the Leichhardt River is the Moondarra Caravan park, 07 4743 9780, with large drive through sites and self-contained air conditioned cabins.

BOATING

There are no boating restrictions and there are four boat ramps around the lake.

Leichhardt River Dam **Lake Moondarra**

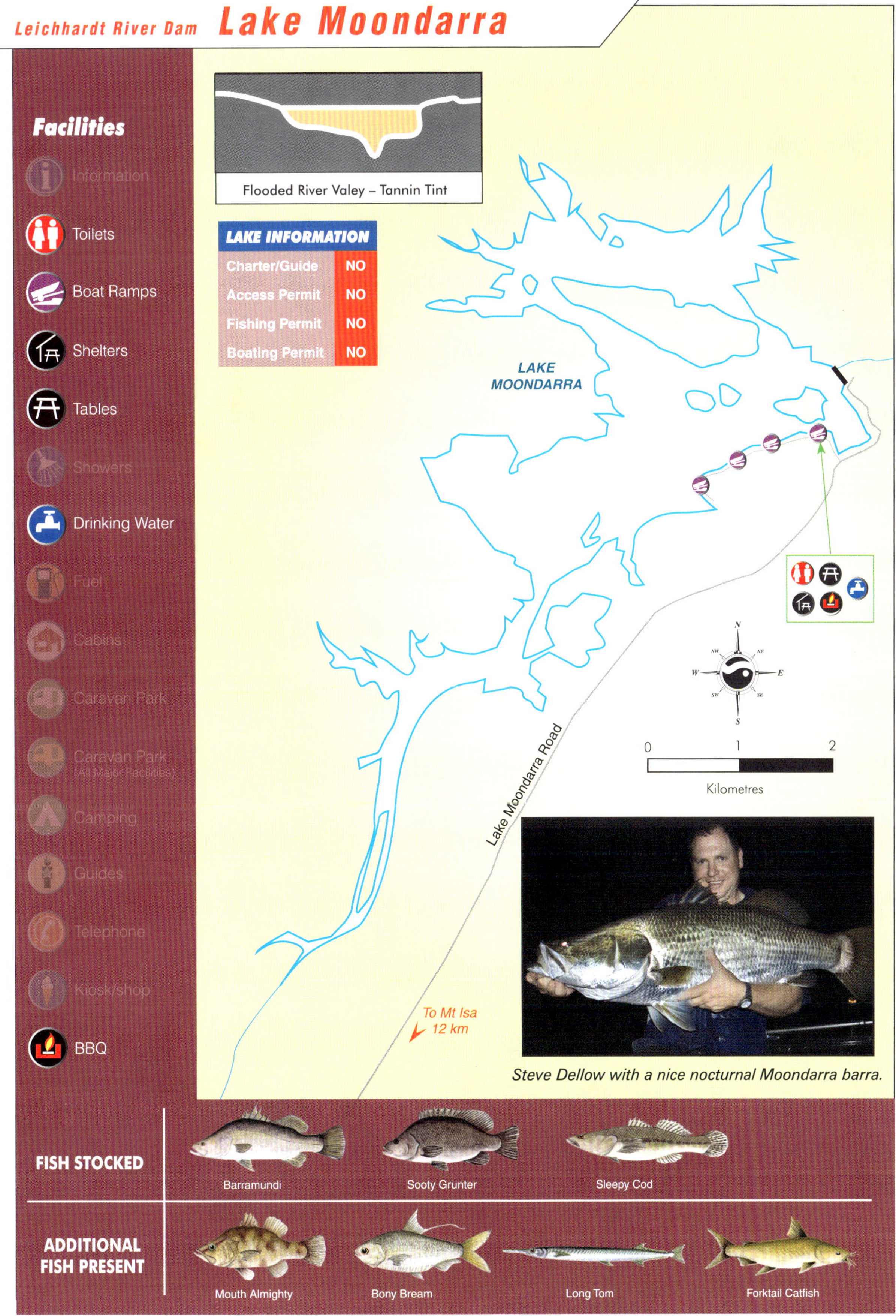

Steve Dellow with a nice nocturnal Moondarra barra.

North Pine Dam

About

Location	Petrie
Drainage	North Pine River System
Surface Area	2200 ha
Capacity	215,000 ML
Usage	Domestic
Management	SEQWC 07 5427 8100

Contact for permit: (Boating) 07 3889 1185 (Fishing inquiries) 0417 742 023

Weipa
Cooktown
CAIRNS
TOWNSVILLE
Mount Isa
Mackay
Rockhampton
Gladstone
Bundaberg
Fraser Island
Birdsville
Maroochydore
BRISBANE
North Pine Dam

Also known as North Pine Dam, this lake is part of the Brisbane water supply grid. As that name suggests, it is built on the northern arm of the Pine River. The Hornibrook Highway bridge crosses the estuary where it enters Moreton Bay near Redcliffe. For years anglers have been excluded from this water, however the Pine Rivers Fish Stocking Association successfully negotiated with the controlling authority to allow (limited) access.

FISHING

For some years, Lake Samsonvale has been producing trophy bass and big yellowbelly. Trolling is the main technique as the designated boating area is devoid of significant fish cover. A single snag near the border of the boating zone gets a hiding. Schooling bass can often be located by trolling and then effectively targeted with cast lures. During winter, these schooling fish often move to shallower water where they can be targeted from the shore. Top lures are soft plastics and blade baits. Saratoga and Mary River cod have also been stocked but will require increased numbers to establish themselves in viable numbers. Schooling juvenile silver perch bite in numbers on bait at times. Bank fishing by the general public is permitted at the Bullocky Rest and MacGavin View recreation areas. Redclaw crayfish have been introduced into the lake along with (illegally) tilapia. Local trends see considerable effort directed at their capture.

Over the years, flooding has allowed plenty of mature fish to escape. During summer and right after floods, the upper Pine River is a haven for monster bass and golden perch. Surface poppers fished right on dusk are winners.

FACILITIES

There are fully appointed picnic facilities at the Bullocky Rest and MacGavin View Recreational Areas. These are very popular at weekends and during holidays. Camping is not permitted. Hotel/motel accommodation is available in Petrie.

BOATING

Boating access is limited to the 200 permit holders who are members the Pine Rivers Fish Stocking Association Inc. as part of their agreement with the Pine Rivers Shire Council. No outboard motors are permitted on the lake.

North Pine Dam has strict limits on boat power and angler numbers.

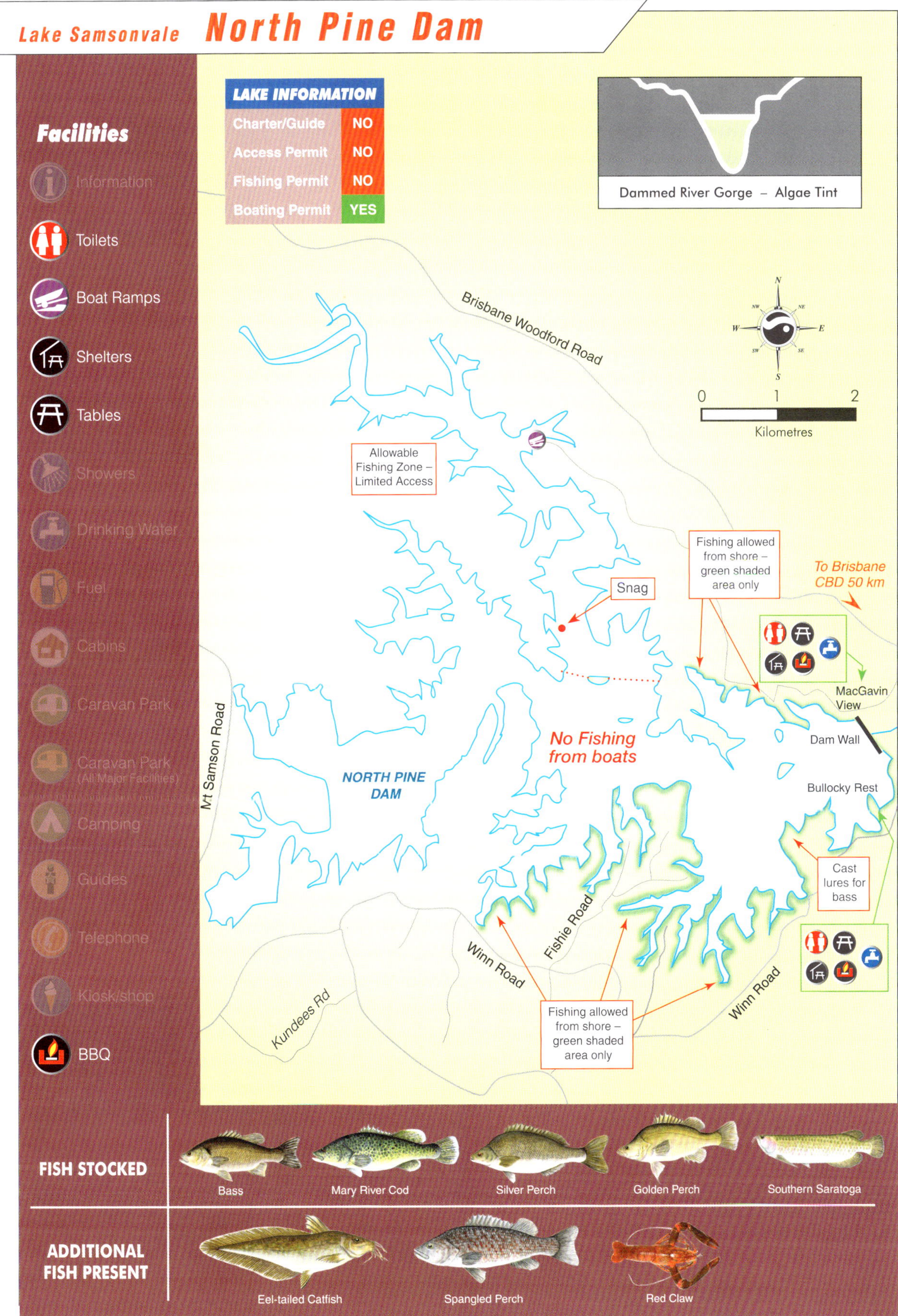
Lake Samsonvale
North Pine Dam
Facilities
Information
Toilets
Boat Ramps
Shelters
Tables
Showers
Drinking Water
Fuel
Cabins
Caravan Park
Caravan Park (All Major Facilities)
Camping
Guides
Telephone
Kiosk/shop
BBQ
LAKE INFORMATION
Charter/Guide NO
Access Permit NO
Fishing Permit NO
Boating Permit YES
Dammed River Gorge – Algae Tint
Brisbane Woodford Road
N
NW
NE
W
E
SW
SE
S
0 1 2
Kilometres
Allowable Fishing Zone – Limited Access
Fishing allowed from shore – green shaded area only
To Brisbane CBD 50 km
Snag
MacGavin View
Dam Wall
No Fishing from boats
Bullocky Rest
Mt Samson Road
NORTH PINE DAM
Cast lures for bass
Fishie Road
Winn Road
Winn Road
Kundees Rd
Fishing allowed from shore – green shaded area only
FISH STOCKED
Bass
Mary River Cod
Silver Perch
Golden Perch
Southern Saratoga
ADDITIONAL FISH PRESENT
Eel-tailed Catfish
Spangled Perch
Red Claw

Paradise Dam

Weipa
Cooktown
CAIRNS
TOWNSVILLE
Mount Isa
Mackay
Rockhampton
Gladstone
Bundaberg
Birdsville
Paradise Dam
Fraser Island
Maroochydore
BRISBANE

About

Location	Biggenden
Drainage	Burnett River
Surface Area	2450 ha
Capacity	300,000 ML
Usage	Agricultural, Industrial & Urban Water
Management	Sun Water 07 4132 6200

Contact for fishing permit: Sun Water

Paradise is waiting for the go ahead to be stocked. A long drawn out court case and fight over the lack of the dam wall providing an effective means for fish migration upstream and down is at the centre of this argument. The tributaries of the Burnett River and the Burnett itself have been stocked above and below the dam. Fish movement is sure to have taken place in the big flood of January 2011 when the water was flowing 6 metres deep over the spillway. There are sure to be some fish living in the dam but a dedicated stocking program will be needed to bolster stocks.

FISHING

At this writing, a stocking and management programme is in advanced stages of planning. As those events unfold, Paradise will participate in the Stocked Impoundment Scheme (SIP) and a permit may be required. The same barra/bass/golden/silver mix already stocked is the likely candidate for future releases.

As the lake fills, shoreline habitat is created. This will receive the attention of casting anglers while the more open reaches will attract trollers. Worth keeping in mind is that recently drowned eucalypts do not fish very well. Live trees whose trunks become deeply submerged go into crisis and try saving themselves with an over-production of sap. This taints the surrounding waters. Fish stay clear. Snags are like good whiskey, they get better with age. The pencil thin sticky bits are better than thick branches. They cure faster and when that happens a coating of algae will grow. This attracts grazing bony bream, which in turn brings the bigger predators.

FACILITIES

Modern visitor facilities include barbecues, picnic shelters, toilets, drinking water and fish cleaning tables. Unpowered campsites are available near the dam wall. Bookings should be made at the kiosk which sells food, ice, bait and fishing tackle. The kiosk is open from Thursday to Monday 07 4127 7278. Powered camping at the top end of the lake can be found at Mingo Crossing 07 4161 6200.

BOATING

There are no boating restrictions. The exclusion zone around the wall that applies to ALL Queensland lakes is clearly indicated. Caution is advised given the numbers of submerging rocks, trees and stumps. A concrete boat ramp is operational while dam levels are high.

Now full, Paradise Dam is a fishery waiting to happen.

Paradise Dam

Facilities at the dam are suitable for launching small to medium sized craft.

Lake Proserpine

Weipa
Cooktown
CAIRNS
TOWNSVILLE
Mount Isa
Lake Proserpine
Mackay
Rockhampton
Gladstone
Bundaberg
Fraser Island
Birdsville
Maroochydore
BRISBANE

About

Location	Proserpine
Drainage	Proserpine River
Surface Area	4325 ha
Capacity	491,400 ML
Usage	Domestic & Industrial
Management	Sun Water Mackay 07 4954 2220

Contact for fishing permit: www.smartservice.qld.gov.au or Sun Water

Peter Faust Dam, also known as Lake Proserpine, contains features that are unique. A big part of the lake can be likened to a championship golf course—so hazard strewn that hackers find it impossible to play. It wasn't happenstance but the hand of Old Hughie. Upon the completion of the main structure, workers typically set about clearing the main basin. While letting their chain saws cool, job half done, enough rain pelted down to float the Ark. The result is that the 'back nine' is a snag city. The inner suburbs contain more sticks—big, small, seen and unseen—than you can poke a barra at. Boats get lost in the timber. In contrast, the main lake basin is as treeless as the Nullarbor.

FISHING (Permit Required)

Clocks can be set on these afternoon sea breezes that funnel up river valleys along much of Australia's east coast The Faust layout is symbolic in that it creates a divide between troller and casters. The latter groups, who rely on stealth, can rejoice in how the sticks slow noisy boats down. Most of them, anyway. Though not visible from the surface, the timbered areas in Faust are criss-crossed by the channels of feeder creeks. These are highways for travelling fish right at the edge. The main basin has shallow points and accompanying weedbeds that shouldn't be ignored.

Faust boasts an excellent barra fishery, with fish over a metre not unusual, together with sooties to over 5 kg. This makes Peter Faust one of Queensland's premier lakes.

FACILITIES

There is no camping at the dam, however just downstream of the dam wall is Camp Kanga, 07 4947 2600, here there are cabins, caravan and camp sites available.

At the dam there are toilets, barbecues, tables, drinking water, shelters and swimming. A ranger is on site.

BOATING

There are no restrictions and a concrete ramp is provided. Hire boats are available from BP Proserpine, 07 4945 3777.

Metre plus barra are relatively common at Lake Proserpine.

Peter Faust Dam Lake Proserpine

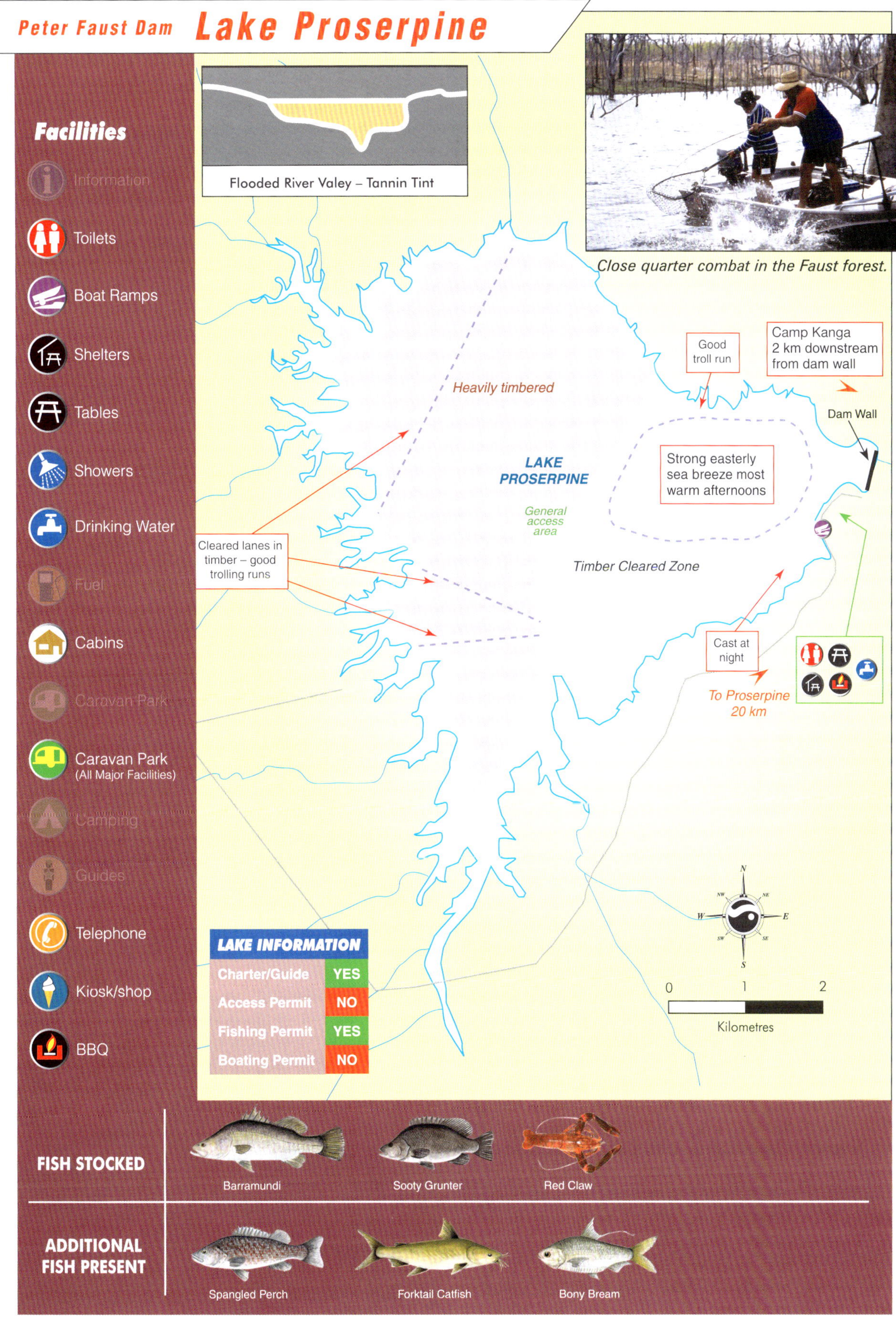

Close quarter combat in the Faust forest.

LAKE INFORMATION	
Charter/Guide	YES
Access Permit	NO
Fishing Permit	YES
Boating Permit	NO

Somerset Dam

Weipa
Cooktown
CAIRNS
TOWNSVILLE
Mount Isa
Mackay
Rockhampton
Gladstone
Bundaberg
Fraser Island
Birdsville
Maroochydore
Somerset Dam
BRISBANE

About

Location	Kilcoy
Drainage	Brisbane
Surface Area	4210 ha
Capacity	910,400 ML
Usage	Domestic & Power Generation
Management	SEQWC 07 5427 8100

Contact for fishing permit: www.smartservice.qld.gov.au & www.seqwater.com.au

Sited in the scenic Brisbane River Valley, a full Somerset Dam contains 30 km of navigable water that produces on a year round basis. Somerset has everything a good lake needs—deep water, rocky points, large flats areas, standing and laying down timber. This array of fish habitat offers something for anglers of every persuasion and experience level. Surveys reveal that Lake Somerset is amongst Queensland's five most fished locations, salt or fresh. A prime spot known in local fishspeak as Queen Street (main street, Brisbane CBD) suggests as much. The lake has northern and southern sealed road accesses via the Cunningham or D'Aguilar Highways.

FISHING (Permit Required)

Though primarily known as a stronghold for trophy bass, Somerset is a rich and diverse fishery that commonly gives up golden perch up to 6 kg and the infrequent Mary River cod that can be 20 kilograms. Lungfish (fully protected) are common in the timbered back blocks, along with a steadily increasing number of saratoga.

Deep schooling bass are a major drawcard to lure casting anglers and fly fishermen from autumn through to spring. Heavily rigged soft plastics, blade baits, soft vibes and ice jigs will usually tempt a few. The heavily pressured bass schools will quickly shut down once a few fish are pinned unless they are having a feeding frenzy. During summer, the schools tend to break up and the bass scatter and suspend in the deeper water making them great trolling targets. Occasionally schools can be found across shallow flats where they love small profile heavy spinnerbaits.

Bait anglers have plenty to keep them occupied, noxious tilapia, having found favour as table fish is a positive incentive for all—and as many as possible is to be gilled and gutted. Freshwater garfish have multiplied into a mega-biomass, easy to catch on simple gear and quite tasty when crispy crunchy fried. Productive lure techniques include trolling, casting to cover and vertical jigging where deep schools are located. Trolling runs follow the old river bed from Queen Street down to 'The Hump' in the lower basin. Bait fishers tie up to trees. Live shrimps are the best bait but involve some effort to procure. Worms can be purchased at bait shops in the near region.

The local fish stocking group is Somerset & Wivenhoe Fish Stocking Assn Inc., PO Box 541, Ipswich, 4305.

FACILITIES

Somerset has two public access points. The Spit has daylight till dark access with facilities that include barbecues, picnic shelters and toilets. The Lake Somerset Holiday Park 07 5497 1184 has a well appointed and maintained camping ground that fills during school holidays. The controlling authority manages facilities that also include a number of ablution blocks, drinking and hot water points. Access to the holiday park and the Kirkleigh area is via security coded boom gates at the entrance. Visitors can check in to get their code or to pay for accommodation at the cabins or campsites. The near region offers motel and farmstay accommodations. Contacts include the Ranger Station 07 5426 0188 and South East Queensland Water Corporation 07 5426 0188.

BOATING

A boating permit is required. These are available at the Kirkleigh Kiosk or the ranger station at the dam wall for $15/week or $100/year. Yearly renewals are $75. There are multi-lane concrete launching ramps at The Spit and Kirkleagh.

Somerset Dam is a regular haunt for anglers targeting trophy bass.

Somerset Dam

Former bass guide Gary Fitzgerald with a nice fish for a lady client from Somerset Dam.

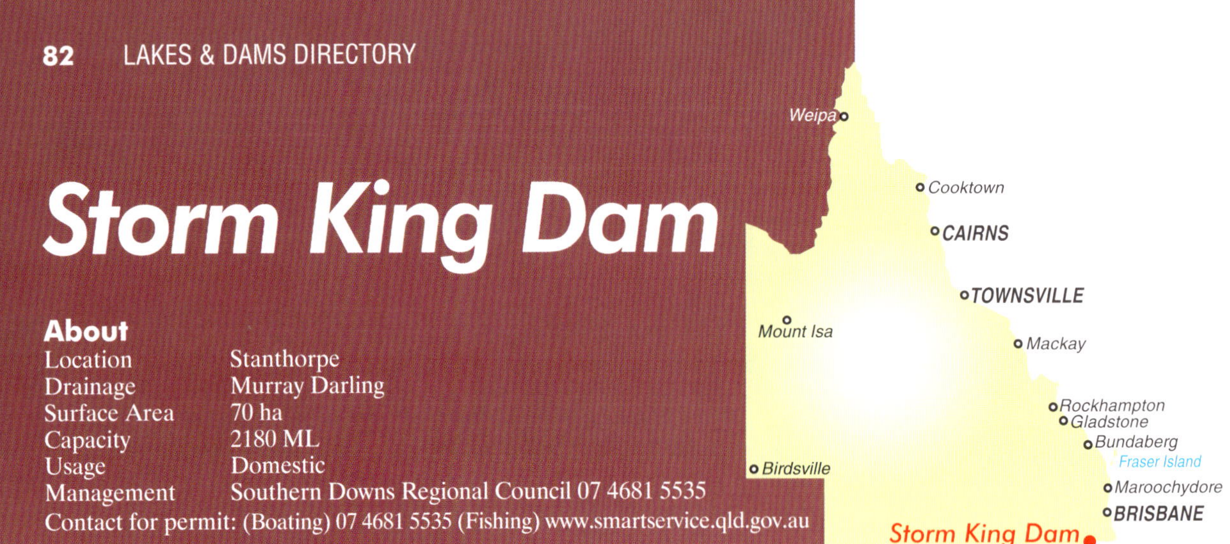

Storm King Dam

About

Location	Stanthorpe
Drainage	Murray Darling
Surface Area	70 ha
Capacity	2180 ML
Usage	Domestic
Management	Southern Downs Regional Council 07 4681 5535

Contact for permit: (Boating) 07 4681 5535 (Fishing) www.smartservice.qld.gov.au

Situated just a few kilometres from Stanthorpe, Storm King Dam offers some good angling opportunities for Murray cod, yellowbelly and silver perch.

FISHING (Permit Required)

While this quiet little pocket of a lake isn't well known to the broader angling community, locals have been partaking of the quality cod and yellowbelly fishing for years. Storm King has a very high stocking density, however fish shelter is limited to the 30 foot lake bed depths near the dam wall and soft weedy cover at the marshy rear of the lake. A rounded, rocky formation not far below the on-site recreational hall is a popular platform for shore based anglers who do well with spinnerbaits when fish are moving. The deepest parts of the lake lay within casting range. The technique is to cast out as far as possible and after allowing the spinnerbait to sink to the bottom, bring it back with a slow roll retrieve.

Boating is limited due to the narrow nature of the lake. Trollers get good fish but put in the time and miles working back and forth, dragging deep running lures that trundle near and along the lake bottom. Storm King is the only Queensland lake that experiences occasional winter snows. A geographic location on the range summit subjects the lake to changeable weather, which, in turn, isn't good for natives. For that reason, Storm King is a location best saved for the sunny days (and still) nights that go with stable weather.

FACILITIES

There are toilets, barbecues, picnic tables and drinking water at the dam. There is no camping at the dam, but there is a recreational camp at the dam is available for group bookings, 07 4681 1920. There is caravan park accommodation at Stanthorpe.

BOATING

Any person wishing to operate a power boat on Storm King Dam should contact Council's Health & Building Services Section on 07 4681 5535 to apply for a permit. As the office is only open from Monday to Friday, it is advised to call ahead if visiting on weekends.

During times of drought, there may be restrictions on the operation of boats on the dam. Further information regarding restrictions can be obtained on the above contact number.

There is a concrete boat ramp.

A typical Murray cod from Storm King Dam.

Storm King Dam

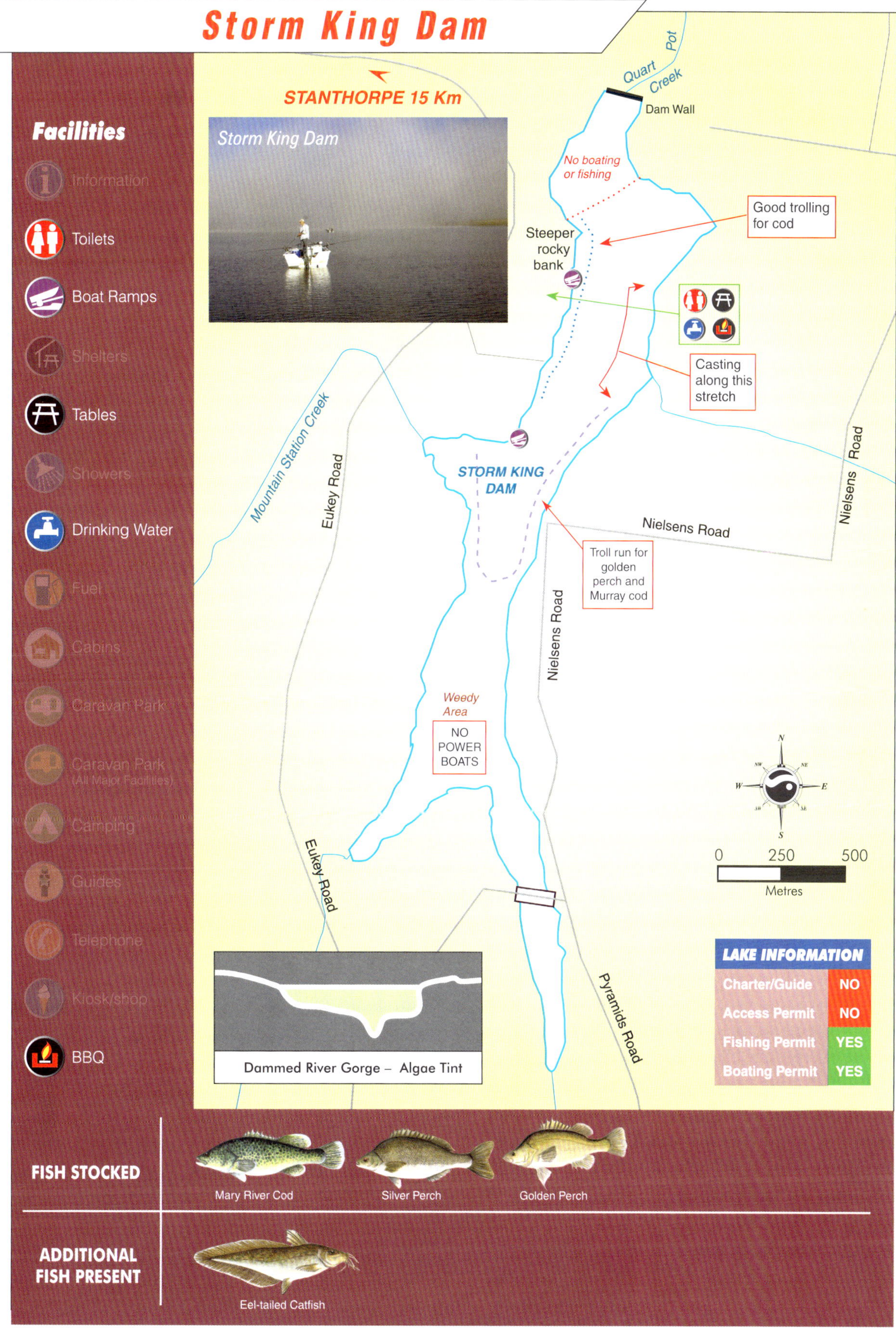

Teemburra Dam

About

Location	Mackay
Drainage	Pioneer River
Surface Area	1040 ha
Capacity	147,200 ML
Usage	Irrigation / Domestic
Management	Sun Water 07 4783 0555

Contact for fishing permit: www.smartservice.qld.gov.au

This dam was constructed in 1997 for town water storage and irrigation purposes. It is located approximately 50 km west of Mackay on a well sealed road. In fact, you would almost pass it if you were going to Eungella Dam.

FISHING (Permit Required)

On the basis of strikes per fishing hour, Teemburra sets the bar. Prior to word getting out and the lake becoming a tournament venue and barra bonanza for locals, hundred fish days happened. Those extraordinary and never to be repeated events resulted from a very dense stocking programme initiated by the well organised and proactive Mackay fish stocking group. Though the bite tempo has slackened somewhat as boat traffic increases along with the conditioning that occurs with the fish living in busy lakes, Teemburra still delivers the goods.

The lake contains varied barra habitat. This includes strands of dead timber and extensive weedbeds that produce spectacularly when fish are rising to shallow minnows and surface lures. Fly fishing with Dahlberg Divers and Silicone Slider type flies is also highly effective. Trolling is an option, however when working open and relatively shallow waters, better results will be achieved though a few simple considerations. Troll on electric motors where possible. Troll with the wind as this minimises wave slap on hulls—a factor that puts fish off. Troll a long way back. This helps remove the boat from the equation. This ploy brings up the question of lure section. What's needed is a type that will max out, depth-wise, without running into the weedy bottom.

Teemburra is also well known for its football shaped sooty grunter. These fish can go into hiding when the big barra are on the prowl. Accurate casts into the tightest structure are often rewarded with rod jarring strikes. Downsized lures or even spinnerbaits can be used to specifically target these fish. When the water is running in, it's definitely worth a look up the top of Teemburra Creek.

FACILITIES

There is no camping allowed at the dam. There are toilets, picnic tables and shelters. There is accommodation some 5 kilometres away at Pinnacle Hotel, 07 4958 5207 and Mirani Caravan Park, 07 4959 1239.

BOATING

A boat motor restriction of 25 hp was removed and now boats with higher horse power can enjoy the Teemburra action. No water skiing is allowed. A single lane concrete ramp is provided.

Downsizing lures can provide some great action on Teemburra's chunky sooty grunter.

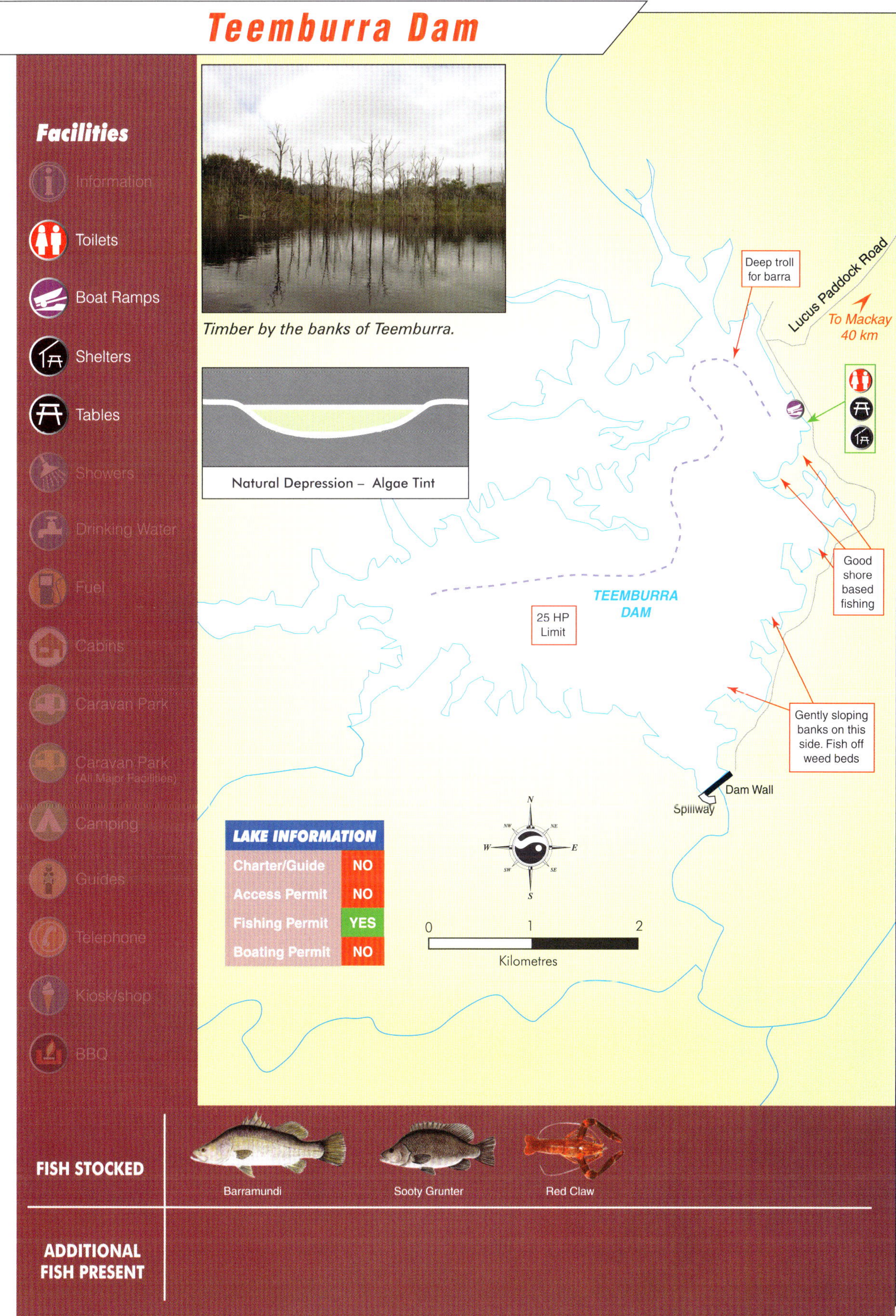
Teemburra Dam
Facilities
Information
Toilets
Boat Ramps
Shelters
Tables
Showers
Drinking Water
Fuel
Cabins
Caravan Park
Caravan Park (All Major Facilities)
Camping
Guides
Telephone
Kiosk/shop
BBQ
Timber by the banks of Teemburra.
Natural Depression – Algae Tint
Deep troll for barra
Lucus Paddock Road
To Mackay 40 km
Good shore based fishing
TEEMBURRA DAM
25 HP Limit
Gently sloping banks on this side. Fish off weed beds
Dam Wall
Spillway
N
NE
E
SE
S
SW
W
NW
0
1
2
Kilometres
LAKE INFORMATION
Charter/Guide NO
Access Permit NO
Fishing Permit YES
Boating Permit NO
FISH STOCKED
Barramundi
Sooty Grunter
Red Claw
ADDITIONAL FISH PRESENT

Theresa Creek Dam

About

Location	Clermont
Drainage	Fitzroy River
Surface Area	300 ha
Capacity	70,000 ML
Usage	Irrigation / Domestic
Management	Belyando Shire Council 07 4983 1133

Contact for fishing permit: N/A

The unsealed road passing through Copperfield village leads to Lake Theresa, another of Queensland's lesser sung, stocked barramundi impoundments. Theresa Creek Dam is located 22 km south west of Clermont in central Queensland.

From day one, Theresa has been a well managed fishery. Prior to any barra liberations, a food source was established in the form of bony bream, which quickly multiplied. The resultant barra growth rates are equal to those of any other lake.

FISHING

While currently this location is hardly mentioned as a fishing destination, it has a big fishing future. Being located well inland, Theresa Creek Dam will be less affected by coastal south-easterly winds that can often put barra in coastal lakes off the bite.

Theresa has its share of metre class trophy barra. The uncluttered lake lends itself to casting and trolling. Visitors take some surprising fish casting from the shore around the picnic area.

Being located at least 300 km from the sea has influences both good and bad. There's a significant lessening of the negative effects of southerly aspect winds that drop surface temperatures and put barra down. However, the further from the coast, the bigger the temperature fluctuations between summer and winter. Theresa temperatures get down the low teens in July. This is under the tolerance threshold of some fish Their well resourced infrastructure maintains an excellent stocking density.

Barrabound visitors heading north along the inland route may well accomplish their mission with a short detour to this pretty and well appointed lake.

FACILITIES

The local stocking group, amongst the most pro-active in the State, has done a wonderful job with visitor facilities. Bush camping is allowed at Lake Theresa, however a permit is required. Permits are available 07 4983 1133. No powered sites are provided. Coin operated barbecues, picnic area, toilets and hot showers are provided, however the water is not fit for human drinking. There is no drinking water on site, so take your own.

Hotel / Motel accommodation provided in Clermont or Emerald.

BOATING

There are no boating restrictions on Lake Theresa and a concrete boat ramp is provided.

Theresa Creek Dam has a number of structural features that hold fish. Weedless surface lures can work well.

Theresa Creek Dam

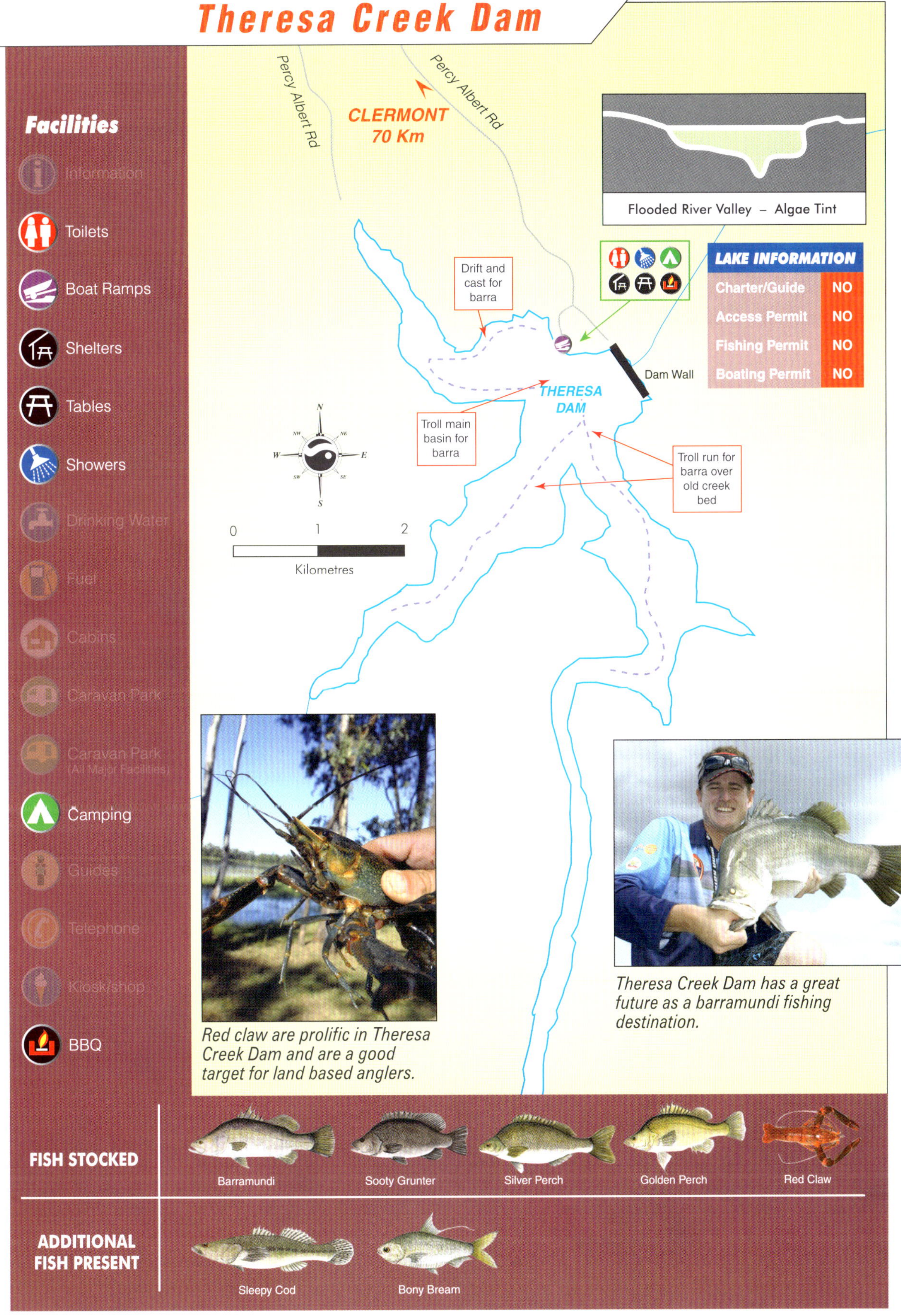

Red claw are prolific in Theresa Creek Dam and are a good target for land based anglers.

Theresa Creek Dam has a great future as a barramundi fishing destination.

Lake Tinaroo

About

Location	Atherton
Drainage	Barron River
Surface Area	3320 ha
Capacity	436,500 ML
Usage	Irrigation
Management	Sun Water

Contact for fishing permit: www.smartservice.qld.gov.au

Built across the Barron River Gorge, Tinaroo Falls Dam is where lake barra stocking all started. Lake Tinaroo extends 15 km upstream with a shoreline of approximately 210 kilometres.

The fortuitous location of the Department of Primary Industries research station at nearby Walkamin earmarked Tinaroo for early barramundi lake releases once hatchery production techniques were perfected. Fingerling releases have since topped the million mark. Some have attained gigantic proportions. A couple of line caught fish have been close to 40 kg and an electrofished specimen temporarily detained in routine scientific sampling went 44 kilograms—about a hundred old fashioned pounds! There are multiple access and launch points.

FISHING (Permit Required)

Fishing species include: archer fish, bony bream, eel-tailed catfish, barramundi, mangrove jack, mouth almighty, northern saratoga, sleepy cod, silver perch, snub nosed gar, sooty grunter and redclaw crayfish. Tilapia were illegally introduced into Lake Tinaroo and have established themselves. This pest species should be destroyed if caught.

The main drawcards to Tinaroo Dam are the sooty grunter (some more than 6 kg) and barramundi (recorded to 45 kilograms).

Specific locations that have a record for producing big barra are the rocky points near the wall, the lily pad filled DPI bay, Tobacco Hill and the ski jump reach of the Barron River arm. A Tinaroo downside, if that's a fitting description, is that Tinaroo sits on a tableland that's 2000 feet above Cairns. A result is clouds collide with mountains with accompanying wind and drizzle... not the sort of conditions that make barra bite. Windows of good fishing are less frequent than on lowland lakes. This advantages the locals with the flexibility to fish whenever the weather is right. In ten years of travelling from Brisbane to Tinaroo, the average was four days in fourteen when confidence of strikes was high. Tinaroo fishes best during the warmer months, and specifically in periods of half light—dusk, dawn and hours between.

FACILITIES

There are numerous camping and/or accommodation sites available around the lake including:
Tinaroo Haven Holiday Lodge Fax 07 3319 7232
Lake Tinaroo Holiday Park Tel 07 4095 8232
Tinaroo Tropical Houseboats Tel 07 4095 8322
Lavender Hill Bed & Breakfast Tel 07 4095 8384
Tinaroo Park Retreat Tel 07 4095 3431
Lake Tinaroo Terraces Tel 07 4095 8555

Other facilities at the lake include toilets, picnic tables, showers, kiosk, public telephone, drinking water, food and fuel.

BOATING

There are no boating restrictions and several concrete boat ramps are available.

Tinaroo barra are big but require a lot of casts. Harro took this one off the bank.

Lake Tinaroo

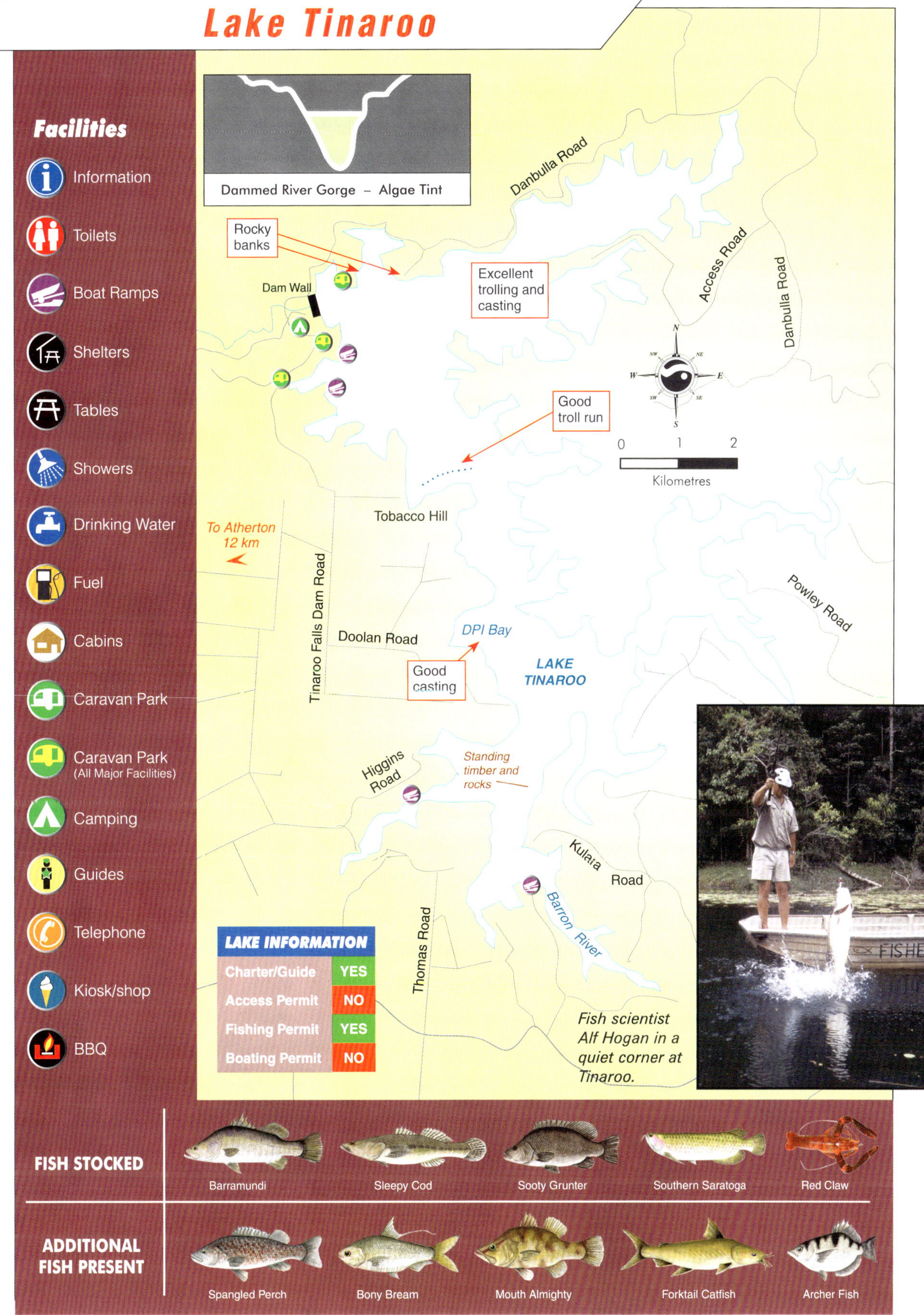

LAKE INFORMATION	
Charter/Guide	YES
Access Permit	NO
Fishing Permit	YES
Boating Permit	NO

Fish scientist Alf Hogan in a quiet corner at Tinaroo.

Wivenhoe Dam

About

Location	Fernvale
Drainage	Brisbane River
Surface Area	10,800 ha
Capacity	1,165,000 ML
Usage	Domestic & Hydro
Management	SEQWC 07 5427 8100

Contact for fishing permit: www.smartservice.qld.gov.au and SEQWC

Named after the British Isles town, Wivenhoe has Saxon origins—wiven a word meaning a name, hoe a reference to a ridge or spur of land. Originally planned as a flood mitigation measure after floods inundated the Brisbane CBD in 1974. After struggling with low water levels, the dam has since filled. Widespread rain in the catchment caused flooding to the Brisbane area in January 2011 when the dam reached 191%. Plenty of bass escaped topping up the existing stocks in the Brisbane River below. When full, this million megalitre lake backs up to the base of the wall of Somerset dam, some 40 km away. Over a million fingerlings have been stocked since it was completed in 1985. The lake terrain is that of rolling hills with a flat and expansive main basin. The shoreline is generally shallow and fringed with weedbeds, the cradle of lake food chains. The eastern rim of the lake has a steeper shore that includes locations like the Platypus Cliffs.

FISHING (Permit Required)

Wivenhoe contains Australia's trophy bass mother lode. More 50+ cm fish come from this vast lake than anywhere else. The background dynamic is a combination of an incalculable forage fish biomass and light fishing pressure. The best bass fishing occurs from May through September when vast schools move into the main basin. A sound approach is to troll small to moderate sized diving lures with 6+ m depth capabilities and, when schools are located, make vertical presentations with bibless vibe types, metal jigs and weighted soft plastics. Spinnerbaits and other sinking lures work well along the deeper waters signposted by cliffs and rocky banks.

Big golden perch and Mary River cod are also encountered. Some saratoga have been stocked. An enormous population of forktail catfish becomes active with the onset of summer and dominates catches through autumn. A self propagating population of silver perch adds variety and zip into the fishing day. The availability of garfish in large numbers and their ease of capture (and the absence of a bag limit) makes them popular. Redclaw crayfish have established and so too, unfortunately, has tilapia.

The local fish stocking group is Somerset & Wivenhoe Fish Stocking Assn Inc., PO Box 541, Ipswich, 4305.

FACILITIES

Public access is controlled by courteous and efficient ranger staff. The lake is open only during daylight hours. Gates are locked overnight at boat launching points at Hamon Cove and Logan Inlet.

Camping is permitted at Captain Logan Camp 07 5426 4729 and Lumley Hill 07 5426 4729, however advance bookings are required and fees apply. Lakeside appointments include toilets, barbecues, public telephone, hot showers, playground, picnic tables, drinking water, limited firewood and a weekend kiosk. A tourist complex at Cormorant Bay includes a restaurant. Contacts include Lake Wivenhoe Information Centre 07 5426 1866.

BOATING

The same SEQWC permit applicable to Lake Somerset applies to Wivenhoe, however all fishing boats are limited to the use of electric motors.

Lake Wivenhoe Information Centre: 07 5426 1866

Lake Wivenhoe is a scenic fishing location that is only a short drive from Brisbane.

Wivenhoe Dam

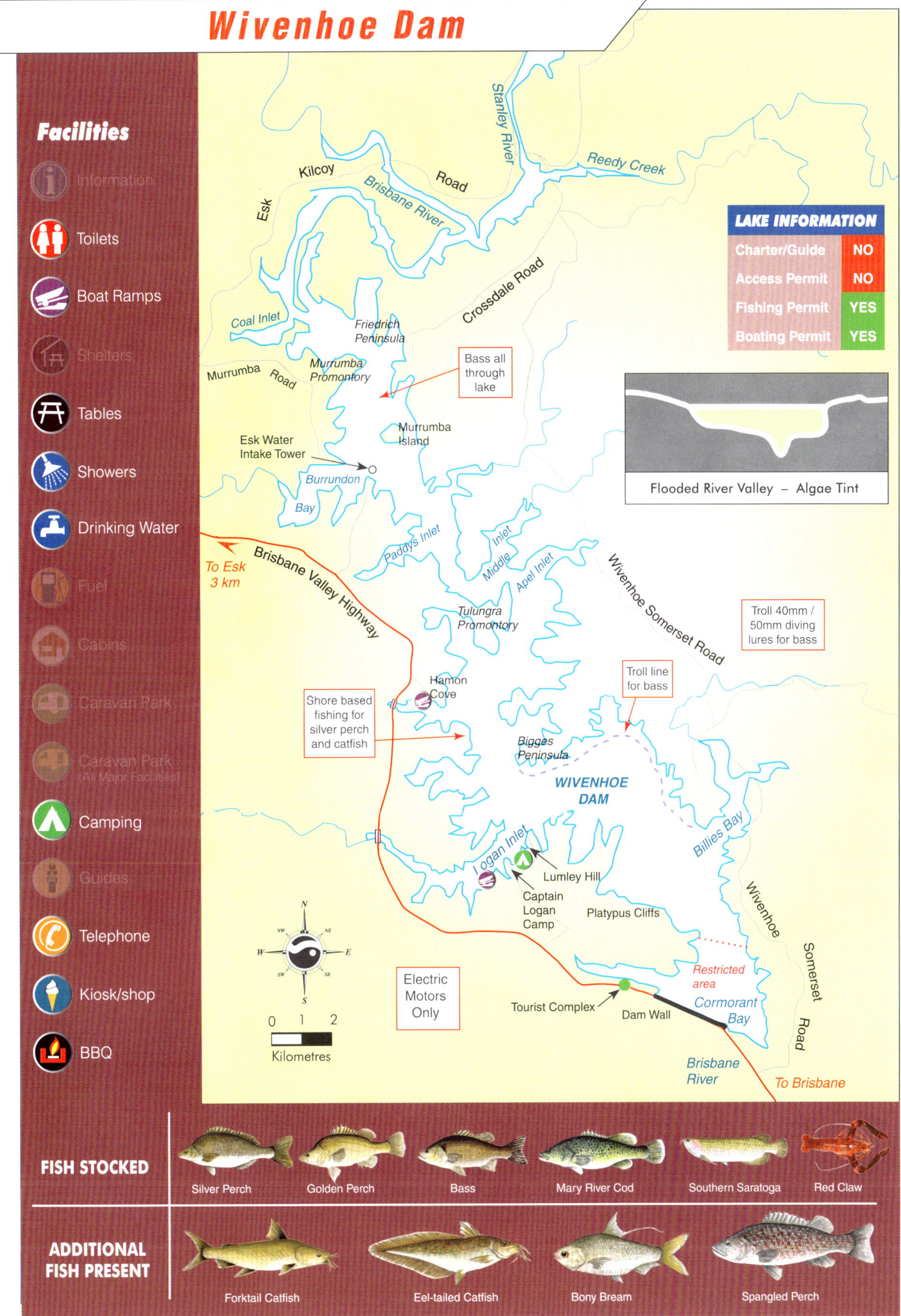

Wuruma Dam

About

Location	Eidsvold
Drainage	Upper Burnett River System
Surface Area	1775 ha
Capacity	165,000 ML
Usage	Irrigation
Management	Sun Water

Contact for fishing permit: www.smartservice.qld.gov.au

This lesser known lake was built in 1968 and contains an attractive sportfish roster. At first glance Wuruma looks a bit of an insubstantial lake—a lake that a good caster could cover in an hour. But first impressions aren't always right, not with fishing. It's not until one takes a boat ride that Wuruma reveals its fuller potential. An attractive section where backed up waters fill a former gorge has enough rocky cover to keep one busy for days.

FISHING (Permit Required)

A mixed fishery has been established with barra, golden perch and Australian bass dominating and trolling is the most popular method amongst a mainly local angler cadre. Being one of the few bass/barra lakes, Wuruma has big potential to draw serious tourism from keen anglers wanting to tangle with two of Australia's premier sports fish targets.

The local stocking group has capitalised on the proximity of the Dawson River as a source of saratoga that are slowly being established in the lake. A large resident eel-tailed catfish population is easily accessed by casual and boatless fisherfolk. An engaging book isn't the thing to take while soaking a bait in that roundish bay just below the camping area. The successive dry years in seasons just past saw Wuruma shrink to a record low before some recovery with the rains of summer '08.

After several small rises, the dam catchment copped a drenching and the dam spilled over at the end of 2010. Even if no fish escaped while the dam was spilling the amount of water between them will make the fishing tougher while the level is high or fish stocks are significantly increased.

Though slightly off the beaten track, but still bitumen all the way, Wuruma awaits discovery by travelling fishermen. An awakening regional tourism infrastructure will most certainly put a little shine on this hidden jewel. Much of the main basin has little in the way of structure but when above about 10–12 per cent of capacity some standing trees become submerged.

FACILITIES

Sparse facilities include picnic shelters, barbecues, drinking water, toilets and cold showers. There is bush camping available, 07 4167 5177 with water views. It is free and there are no pre-bookings required.

BOATING

There are no restrictions and there is a single boat launching ramp. A 200 metre no boating zone exists from the dam wall.

Wuruma Dam hit capacity in the 2010 season rains.

Wuruma Dam

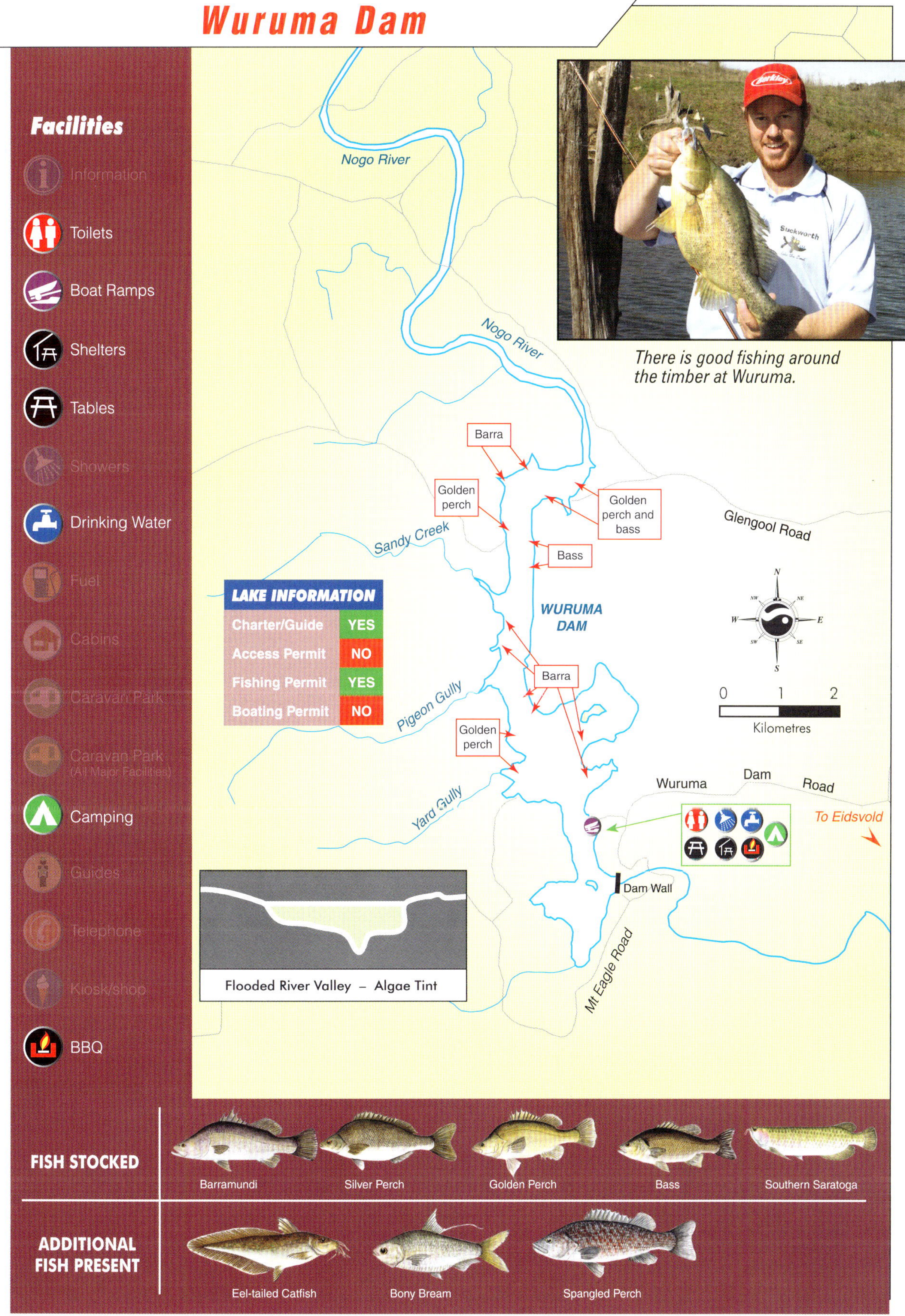

LAKE INFORMATION	
Charter/Guide	YES
Access Permit	NO
Fishing Permit	YES
Boating Permit	NO

There is good fishing around the timber at Wuruma.

CHAPTER ELEVEN

Weirs & Barrages

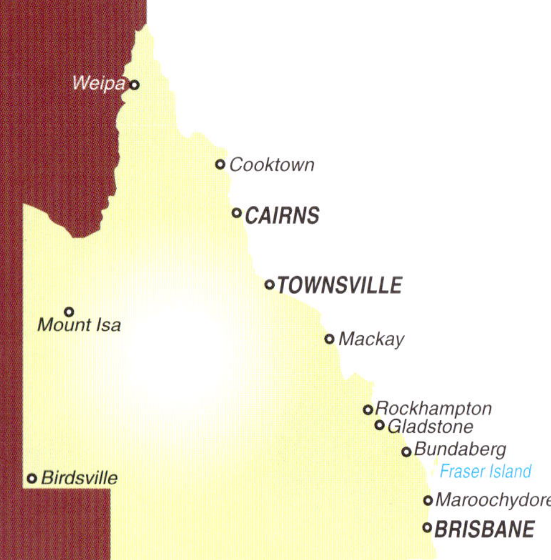

THE BORDERLANDS

The Dumaresq and Macintyre are upper Darling River tributaries. At various stages between Tenterfield and Mungindi, those waters comprise the NSW/Qld border. The Dumaresq River officially starts at the junction the Mole and Severn rivers, extending westwards where it is joined by Macintyre Brook before joining the Macintyre River upstream from Goondiwindi. The Macintyre rises in the westward edge of the New England tableland near Inverell. From a confluence with the Dumaresq, it extends to a junction with the Boomi River below Mungindi, thereafter called the Barwon.

Along both sides signposted Travelling Stock Reserves (TSR) provide river access. A New South Wales fishing license is required whenever fishing from the New South Wales side. A number of weirs offer access from both States and provide limited facilities.

BONSHAW WEIR 35 HA

This popular picnic spot is situated on the Dumaresq near the Bruxner Highway small town of Bonshaw. There is a camping area and toilets on the New South Wales side. The best fishing happens on the upstream side where the deeper water holds more fish. Small boats can be launched above the weir using 4WD vehicles. There is no vehicle or boat access on the downstream side due to a fence across the river.

CUNNINGHAM WEIR 30 HA

Located near Beebo township, Cunningham Weir is also on the Dumaresq River and has a camping area but no facilities. By far the best fishing option is via small craft launched by a 4WD vehicle. Good holes are to be found both side of the structure.

The Macintyre Brook feeds into Coolmunda Dam. On the downstream side, before joining the Dumaresq River there are some prime locations.

GREENUP WEIR

This is an old wooden terraced structure that, when full, backs water up to the causeway below the Coolmunda Dam spillway. It is well stocked with native fish that are reducing plague levels of carp. Small craft can be launched above the weir by 4WD vehicle.

WHETSTONE WEIR

Another fishy location on Macintyre Brook, Whetstone Weir is sited near the township of the same name on the Cunningham Highway. The backed up water is regularly stocked and takes in a reliable local spot known as 'The Pocket'. This location is characterised by undercut banks, standing snags, shady overhangs and deep water—fishy features all. Bush camping is allowed. Picnic tables and barbecue plates are provided. Small craft can be launched with a 4WD vehicle.

GOONDIWINDI

The Gunsynd town offers a 15 km stretch of backed up water that's not only well stocked, but which can be accessed from well appointed picnic grounds just a walk from the main street. This stretch of the Macintyre extends between two weirs and is very popular with trollers. Water skiers make their presence known on summer weekends.

WESTERN QUEENSLAND WEIRS

Town weirs have been erected along the Condamine, Balonne, Culgoa, Warrego, and Paroo—Darling River tributaries meandering through the black soil plains of south western Queensland, and on the Bulloo Rive at Thargomindah.

From a source near Warwick, the Condamine meanders for over 500 km to the town of Surat to become the Balonne. The river forks near Dirranbandi, the main feeder becomes the Culgoa—though more water flows into the storage lakes at Cubbie Station than goes into the Darling. One day there may be an enquiry into the circumstances surrounding the cotton giant but don't expect to see it without the hammer and tong opposition of Cubbie's National Party champions Queensland MP Howard Hobbs and Senator Barnaby Joyce. The summer rains of '08 saw the Condamine at its highest levels in living memory.

The pools created by town weirs and adjacent facilities offer travellers peaceful and shady surrounds in which to wet a line and have a cuppa. Unfortunately, vigilance needs to extend beyond the rod tip. The social cost of youth unemployment and substance abuses has seen increasing smash and grab incidents on vehicles belonging to tourist folk. Police hierarchies these days do not embrace the problem with the same alacrity they have for revenue raising speed traps. So keep an eye out. The days are gone when vehicles could be left on the riverbank, keys in the ignition.

The native fish in these flatland weirs breed more successfully than cousins of the big hill country impoundments. Natural recruitment is bolstered by yellowbelly, silver perch and Murray cod fingerling seedings undertaken by regional fish stocking associations. Though generally muddy, some weirs to be mentioned clear sufficiently for lures to be used with confidence.

TALGAI WEIR 640 ML 37 HA

A small, shallow weir on the Condamine near Clifton. No facilities, gravel launching ramp.

DALBY WEIR 900 ML 52 HA

This weir across Myall Creek is sited amid Dalby parklands and forms a 2.5 km stretch of backed up water suitable for small boats.

CHINCHILLA WEIR 10,000 ML 350 HA

Located a few clicks south of town, Chinchilla Weir when full backs up several miles of excellent lure fishing water. While yellowbelly dominate catches, there are good numbers of quality Murray cod and silver perch. Fish habitat includes abundant standing and fallen timber and fringe weedbeds. Amenities include picnic tables and concrete boat ramp.

GILL WEIR 1050 ML 18 HA

Named after Vince Gill, the former Bjelke Petersen era politician who pushed through the Murray cod introduction into Fairbairn Dam, this structure is built across Dogwood Creek, famed yellowbelly water that joins the Condamine near Surat. Gill Weir is regularly stocked with golden perch and Murray cod. An outboard motors limit of 10 hp applies.

NEIL TURNER WEIR 2000 ML 90 HA

Built across the Maranoa River within walking distance of the town of Mitchell, this natural fishery is supplemented with regular stockings of golden perch and Murray cod. It is open to boating but is badly silted in places.

SURAT WEIR 600 ML 30 HA

Weirs & Barrages of Queensland

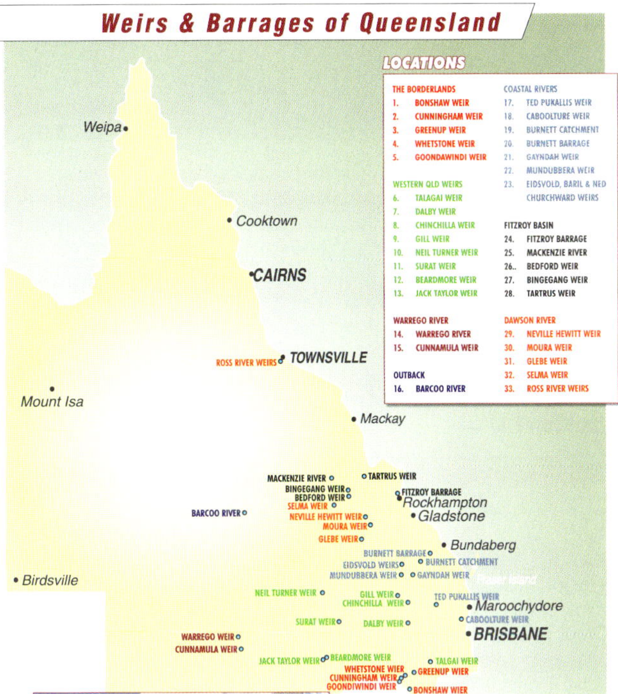

This is good water in the Surat township. Naturally occurring fish stocks are regularly boosted with stocked Murray cod, golden and silver perch fingerlings. Stocking activity also occurs at Gundi Lagoon, a water 40 km from town that fills from Youngerman Creek, a Balonne tributary. A settled nature and plentiful snag and weedbed habitat makes Gundi Lagoon a lure fishing hotspot when full. A small boat is essential and back launching is available.

BEARDMORE DAM 82,000 ML 3350 HA

As is the custom for some, not all, man made Queensland lakes, this body of water is known as Lake Kajarabie was formed in 1972 with the construction of a weir across the junction of the Balonne and Maranoa rivers. Built for town water and irrigation, Kajarabie is a generally shallow lake in which native fish will spawn. When full, it backs up the Balonne for over 70 km and the Maranoa for nearly 20 kilometres. Turbidity rules out lures throughout most of this water, however there are stretches along upper parts of the Balonne arm that can provide superlative sportfishing on spinnerbaits and ilk when dry conditions have been prevailing.

JACK TAYLOR WEIR 10,000 ML 310 HA

Built in 1953 as a town water supply, the Jack Taylor weir backs up a 20 km stretch of the Balonne river below Beardmore Dam. Yet another natural fishery supplemented by releases of Murray cod, golden perch and silver perch. It is an exceptionally productive fishery that offers excellent lure fishing.

WARREGO RIVER

The Warrego River is the northernmost Darling tributary. It rises along the western fall of the Carnarvon Gorge and joins its parent near Bourke. Perennially muddy, it nevertheless holds good yellowbelly and Murray cod stocks. Stocking projects initiated at Charleville bolster the natural recruitment. The Warrego is one of the last rivers where silver perch still naturally breed, water quality issues caused by cotton growing have devastated stocks down river.

Between Charleville and Augathella there are a number of access points. Typically they are called the 'ten mile' the 'eighteen mile' and the 'twenty seven mile'. Those distances come from the antiquity of local folklore and possess the wavering accuracy of country miles. Camping is an option at those spots but the unwritten law is to leave only footprints.

Bakers Bend is a legendary hole that's reached via a turnoff 37 km south of Charleville heading towards Cunnamulla. A dirt track of 5 km leads from the highway to the river. According to old timers from those parts, Bakers Bend holds water through the most severe of dry times. It's a matter of simple logic that during the droughts that reduce rivers like the Warrego and Paroo to intermittent holes that fish instinctively retreat to the deepest water available.

A couple of Warrego feeders are worth a try following wet years. These are Quilberry Creek and the Ward River. Both lay to the west of Charleville and are reached via the Diamantina Development Road. The aboriginal word quilberry means plenty of water. The Ward River has a public reserve 20 km from town, a popular venue used by the local fish stocking association for their annual competition. This event is a fundraiser for fingerlings purchase.

CUNNAMULLA WEIR 4500 ML 155 HA

The backed up water formed by this weir is permanently muddy and snag ridden. As such it is prime yellowbelly habitat that also produces Murray cod.

OUTBACK

'On the upper Barcoo, where churches are few'—I'm not sure whether Banjo was referring to the one bible township of Jericho, but it is amongst the region's historical landmarks. And if not redemption, then certainly a feed of yellowbelly is to be found in the nearby Jordan River. Jericho's Hallelujah Hotel is an establishment that may be as close to heaven as it gets. The Jordan links with the Barcoo of which Slim Dusty rejoices—'catching yellowbelly in the muddy old Barcoo'.

The Alice is another Barcoo feeder that's been restocked. Five kilometres south of Barcaldine along the road to Blackall there's a turnoff to a weir with limited camping facilities, which include a rainwater tank for drinking water, an artesian bore tap for washing, barbecue pits and tables, and two composting toilets. Yellowbelly and Barcoo perch are the fishing staple there.

The Barcoo at Isisford clears sufficiently during dry spells for spinnerbaits and bladed lures to work. The Trafalgar Hole, about 100 km upstream from the Barcoo confluence with Cooper Creek is an exceptional hole. Access and camping is available through Welford National Park.

The lingering Queensland legislative ad hocery that's seen adjacent landholders assume ownership of waters passing through their lands poses access problems in places. Not that they can be blamed the way some people abuse the privilege with their rubbish.

COASTAL RIVERS

Barrages have been erected across a number of coastal rivers. Their purpose is twofold—to block the intrusion of brackish tidal waters and to establish a freshwater pool for regional domestic/rural supply. The combination of increased depth and bankside habitat has earmarked barrages as ideal locations for fingerling releases. Those same features are angler magnets. Bass and barramundi are the logical subjects for seedings.

TED PUKALLUS WEIR

Situated on Cooyar Creek, a Brisbane River feeder above Wivenhoe dam, this attractive water can be viewed from the D'Aguilar Highway between the towns of Kilcoy and Yarraman. Access is via private property. Regular bass stockings are made and it is probable that when water conditions permit, a summertime movement occurs into those parts by bass belonging to the Wivenhoe mother lode.

CABOOLTURE RIVER WEIR

An old fashioned structure that backs up the river in and above urban Caboolture, a name derived from the aboriginal words kabul tur, meaning place of the carpet snake. This attractive habitat is small craft navigable for some distance and was been stocked with silver perch in the 1980s. In more recent years bass have been liberated. It also holds a resident eel-tailed catfish population.

BURNETT CATCHMENT

Rising in the Bunya Mountains and meeting the sea at Bundaberg, the Burnett River catchment drains an extensive area of lower central Queensland.

BURNETT BARRAGE 22,250 ML 625 HA

The Ben Anderson Barrage, as the Bundaberg structure is also known, was built in 1976. It was heavily stocked with bass in 1999, and in years since, with barramundi, saratoga, golden perch and silver perch. Since then, the floods of 2010/2011 have topped the lower Burnett River up with fish stocks from Cania, Boondooma, Wuruma, Paradise and the river between. The location has picnic facilities electric barbecues and a concrete boat ramp.

GAYNDAH WEIR 12,500 ML 365 HA

Also known as Claude Wharton Weir, this structure on a Burnett feeder was built in 1987 and is a short durance from Gayndah township. It has been stocked with bass, golden perch, silver perch and saratoga. Picnic facilities and a concrete boat ramp are amongst appointments.

MUNDUBBERA WEIR 3700 ML 170 HA

Also called Jones Weir this structure on the Burnett River near Mundubbera township dates back to the 1950s. It contains a natural population of spangled perch and ell-tailed catfish and has been stocked with bass, golden perch, silver perch and saratoga. There are picnic facilities and a concrete boat ramp.

EIDSVOLD, BARIL AND NED CHURCHWARD WEIRS

These are supplementary 25,000 ML class storages in various stages of planning and construction along the Burnett River above Paradise Dam. As they come on line barramundi and (probably) saratoga stockings will commence.

FITZROY BASIN

The Fitzroy is the largest river system along the entire east coast. From where it flows into Keppel Bay downstream from Rockhampton, it forks near the cattle town of Dauringa to form the Mackenzie and Dawson rivers. Both are major rivers that drain catchments and, though not as mountainous as, say the Clarence and Hawkesbury, cover vastly bigger areas. Floods following cyclonic rains in February '08 saw an outpouring from the Fitzroy that would exceed any volume in living memory to go down the Murray-Darling.

The Fitzroy basin contains Australia's most diverse mix of freshwater fish. These include barramundi. The naturally occurring population in the lower reaches is augmented by fingerlings releases in upper parts of the system. A separate genetic strain of golden perch has evolved.

Sooty grunter were released into the northern end of the catchment at Funnel Creek. From there they have established and spread ever steadily southward into the Connors, Isaac and Mackenzie rivers. The McKenzie and Dawson rivers, the main Fitzroy feeders offer excellent fishing that's not widely known outside those districts. There are numbers of locations where public access is available that are well appointed with boat launching and picnic facilities.

FITZROY BARRAGE 61,000 ML 1410 HA

This backed up water is visible from the highway as one passes through the town. Facilities include a dual concrete boat ramp and picnic facilities. Forktail catfish comprise the bulk of catches, however a barramundi component alters that balance as travelling fish pass through a modern fishway that has been erected at the barrage.

A situation that should never be allowed to happen saw the barrage go under in floods of recent years. Rocky's rag-tag licensed barramundi netters were on hand to snare the rewards with daily five ton hauls—fish put into the system through the sweat and dedication of anglers wanting to better their life. The Fitzroy has the potential to become Australia's foremost barramundi river and a tourist goldmine, were the netting to be stopped.

MACKENZIE RIVER

This river runs northwards through cattle country to sources on the west side of the coastal ranges inland from Mackay.

Taking in Mackenzie tributaries, Isaac and Connor rivers and Funnel creek, this part of the Fitzroy system holds over 400 km of fishable water. It contains saratoga, golden perch and sooty grunter and from 1997 onwards has been stocked with barramundi.

BEDFORD WEIR 23,000 ML

This water is 30 km north of Blackwater has a concrete ramp and picnic facilities. It is stocked with barramundi but is popular with rev-head water skiers. Camping at the weir is permitted.

BINGEGANG WEIR 12,000 ML

This beautiful stretch of water near Middlemount is characterised by melaleuca clumps growing out of the water. In the main it contains saratoga, barramundi and golden perch. Launching is via an unsealed ramp. There are no facilities.

TARTRUS WEIR 10,000 ML

Access to this 'out of the way' location on the Mackenzie to the south west of Marlborough township requires some local knowledge. Once one departs the Bruce Highway, helpful road signs become scarce. A track departing near Marlborough leads to Tartrus Weir. Besides stocked barramundi, there are saratoga and yellowbelly.

DAWSON RIVER

The Dawson River is steeped in fishing folklore with tales of bulldust and corrugated roads leading to remote fishing holes and the associated big fish tales. The naturally occurring and still present saratoga are locally called spotted barramundi and Dawson River barramundi.

There is a series of six weirs along the section of the Dawson River. These extend between the towns of Baralaba and Taroom, a distance in 'river miles' of approximately 500 kilometres. The main stretch of interest to anglers is encompassed by Neville Hewitt and Glebe weirs. This water has a population of southern strain saratoga, golden perch, silver perch, forktailed catfish, eel-tailed catfish and sleepy cod. The saratoga fishery peaks during the summer months along the snaggier reaches higher in the system. With a table quality that can be safely called inedible, these spotted leapers nevertheless have an attitude that catch and release fly and lure anglers appreciate. Regional preferences however, are more slanted towards yellowbelly with good catches possible, especially below the weirs when a rise pours over the spillway. Angling from the bank with bait is the preferred local method.

NEVILLE HEWITT WEIR 11,500 ML

Also called Baralaba Weir, Neville Hewitt Weir contains excellent fishing. It was stocked with 15,000 barramundi fingerlings in 1999. Golden perch fingerling releases totalled 20,000 in 1996 and 22,500 in 1999. Fishing restrictions apply within 400 metres of the weir and to the downstream side of the bridge on the Baralaba/Woorabinda Road.

MOURA WEIR 7250 ML

First stocked with barramundi in 2000. Facilities include toilets, picnic tables and wood fire barbecues. Boat launching is via a concrete ramp.

GLEBE WEIR 17,500 ML

Stocked yearly with golden perch since 1995 with 40,000 fingerlings released in 1998 and 17,500 in 2000. Picnic facilities and concrete boat ramp available

SELNA WEIR

Also called Emerald Weir and built on the Nogoa River within walking distance of the CBD. It is well stocked with barramundi and very popular with local anglers and has launching facilities for small boats.

ROSS RIVER WEIRS

This three weir chain extends downstream from the Ross River Dam, Townsville's water supply. Fishing is not permitted there, however anglers are free to come and go at any time in those downstream. Located within city limits these locations are popular with youngsters able to ride their bikes there. Noted fishing guide Steve Jeston frequently fished Aplins Weir as a kid. Summer evenings would find him paddling his canoe, lure in tow.

All are heavily stocked with barramundi, that program having the enthusiastic support of civic authorities aware of the very high proportion of kids who fish being immune to the peer pressures that lead to drugs and hooning in cars.

Black Weir contains 250 ML covering 85 hectares.

Gleeson Weir contains 44 ML and extends over 15 hectares.

Aplins Weir has a 220 ML capacity and an area of 64 hectares. Aplins produces barramundi to 20 kg on a regular basis. Tidal waters intrude to the foot of the dam wall. Lurecasting anglers fishing the top of the tide from rocks below the dam wall make some surprising catches that include barra, tarpon, mangrove jack, queenfish and giant herring.

DESIGNED FOR FISH

BUILT FOR CARE

RIVERPRO

Ideal for the river or the ocean. Thanks to the handle and the floating structure, it can be recovered in case of accidental release.

DELUXE FLOATING FOLDING NET S

Deluxe Floating Folding 40CM with telescopic handle including belt clip. Folds down to 10 cm to fit in a standard net scabbard.
This net is ideal for all small fish including trout, bream, golden perch, whiting, flathead. The PVC rubber coated net is Fish Friendly.

Telescopic handle	**35cm – 50 cm**
Hoop Size	**40 cm X 40 cm**
Overall Length	**90 cm**
Net Depth	**25 cm**
Folded Length	**8 cm X 40 cm**

AC0535

DELUXE FLOATING NET S

Deluxe Floating Foldable 40CM NET with telescopic handle including belt clip.
This net is ideal for all small fish including bream, trout, golden perch, whiting, flathead. The PVC rubber coated net is Fish Friendly

Telescopic handle	**37cm – 65 cm**
Hoop Size	**40 cm X 30 cm**
Overall Length	**105 cm**
Net Depth	**25 cm**
Folded Length	**30 cm X 45 cm**

AC9478

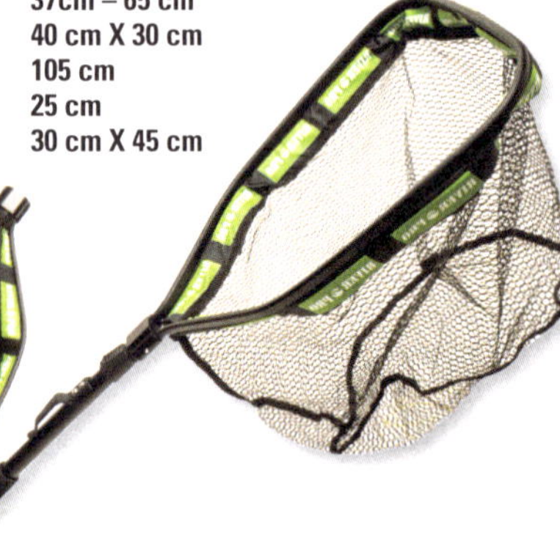

FLOATING - 3 PIECE TELESCOPIC NET

AFN Fishing & Outdoors is proud to introduce the latest innovation in angling gear: the SEA PRO Floating 3-Piece Telescopic Fish Landing Net. Designed for versatility, durability, and ease of use, this premium landing net is a game-changer for land-based anglers fishing in both saltwater and freshwater environments.

Telescopic handle	**3m**
Hoop Size	**50 cm X 50 cm**
Folded length	**100 cm**

AC1211

- *3-piece telescopic handle – Extends to 3 metres, collapses to 100 cm*
- *Floating design – Never lose your net in the water*
- *Corrosion-resistant aluminum frame – Lightweight and durable*
- *Fish-friendly knotless mesh – Protects fish and reduces damage*
- *Net width: 50 cm, Net depth: 50 cm – Ideal for various species*
- *Perfect for land-based fishing – Piers, high banks, and rocky shores*

DELUXE FLOATING NET M

Deluxe Floating Foldable 50CM NET with telescopic handle including belt clip.
This net is ideal for all small to medium fish including bream, trout, Murray cod, golden perch, whiting, flathead. The PVC rubber coated net is Fish Friendly

Telescopic handle	**65cm – 95 cm**
Hoop Size	**50 cm X 40 cm**
Overall Length	**150 cm**
Net Depth	**40 cm**
Folded Length	**50 cm X 65 cm**

AC9485

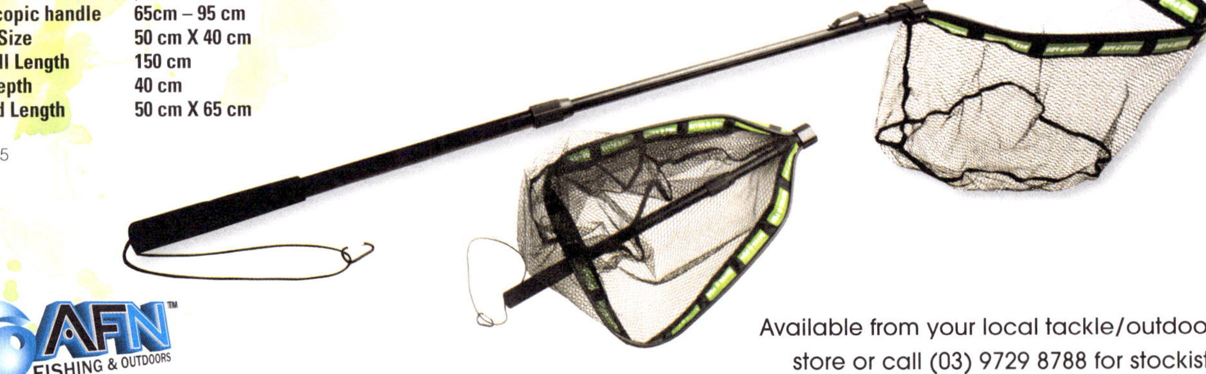

AFN FISHING & OUTDOORS

Available from your local tackle/outdoors store or call (03) 9729 8788 for stockists!